Barbados

Footprint

Sarah Cameron

Contents

Listings

About the author

After a degree in Latin American Studies Sarah Cameron has been travelling and writing on the continent ever since, both as an economist and as an author for Footprint Handbooks. Initially moonlighting for the *South American Handbook* while working for a bank, in 1990 she parted company with the world of finance and has been contributing to the expansion of Footprint titles ever since. Sarah now concentrates solely on the Caribbean and is the author of *Footprint Caribbean Islands* as well as individual island titles. When she is not travelling around the Caribbean sampling beaches and rum cocktails, she retreats to her 17th-century farmhouse in rural Suffolk.

Tourism and Barbados go together like rum and coke or flying fish and chips. Visitors turn up time and time again, tune into the rhythm of calypso, soca and reggae and chill out with a *Mount Gay* rum or *Banks* beer. You can pay thousands of dollars to be seriously pampered alongside tanned music moguls and svelte supermodels, or forego life's more indulgent pleasures by catering for yourself and shopping with local Bajans. The west coast, commonly referred to as the Platinum coast for the wealth of its guests, is the place to see and be seen. The south coast has the best beaches and is a popular choice for the package holiday end of the market, with a cheerful, relaxed atmosphere by day and nocturnal fun and games. The east is wild and untamed, a world apart, where the Atlantic crashes into cliffs, eroding the coastline and creating beaches of rare beauty. Drag yourself away from the coast though, into the hills inland to explore relics of colonial days such as plantation houses and signal towers, lush tropical gardens, museums and – you've guessed it – rum distilleries.

Don't look back

Of all the islands in the eastern Caribbean, Barbados stands apart as the one that remained British throughout its colonial history, instead of being passed from one European master to another. Some towns have charming English seaside resort names: Hastings, Brighton or Dover, while administratively the country is organized into parishes, reflecting the overwhelming Anglican influence. In the past it was often referred to as Little England, and not always as a compliment. Since independence in 1966 the country has been trying to shake off that white middle class suburban image and has moved closer in cultural terms to North America while also pursuing its African roots from the days of the slave trade. Trafalgar Square has been renamed in honour of national heroes and the statue of Lord Nelson, a supporter of slavery, has been turned round so that he no longer looks down Broad Street. But some old habits die hard. You can still go to a polo match and be offered tea and cucumber sandwiches, or watch Sunday cricket on the village green. A Test Match at the Kensington Oval, though, is a different kettle of flying fish and an example of how an English sport has been turned into pure Afro-Caribbean pageantry, with an exuberant audience adding drums, whistles, masks and costumes.

Island rhythm

Bajans stress their Afro-Caribbean heritage and have developed it in their music and festivals. Drum music, which was banned by colonial masters to prevent the organization of rebellions, is thumped out all over the island and 'tuk' bands are an essential part of carnival processions. Reggae, too, has its own enthusiastic fans and many home-grown professional exponents. Calypso, soca and pan music blast from cars and bars, as well as being the centrepiece of Crop Over, the boisterous festival celebrating the end of the sugar harvest. Rhythm is in the Barbadian blood. Even baby Bajans can dance better than the average white tourist.

At a glance

South coast

The south coast is the liveliest part of the island with deep sandy beaches, wall-to-wall hotels for those on a lower budget, watersports and nightlife. Entertainment here is less 'tasteful' than on the west coast, more boisterous, with reggae and steel pan music thumping on every corner, but that needn't stop you liming (chilling) with the locals under a shady tree. Some of the best beaches are Silver Sands, Miami Beach and Accra Beach in Christ Church parish, and Long Bay, Bottom Bay, Foul Bay, Crane Beach, Harrismith and Sam Lord's in St Philip.

Bridgetown and around

Bridgetown, the capital, is the commercial heart of the island. The Careenage, where shipping used to dock, is the focal point of the city and most of the older buildings are clustered around the waterway. Nowadays catamarans and fishing boats for day trips tie up in front of bars and restaurants while old warehouses are being converted. Broad Street is stuffed with jewellers, boutiques, department stores and duty-free shops but for a more Bajan feel stroll along Swan Street where the locals do their shopping. The architecture is a mix of Victorian and 20th-century ranging from the Parliament Buildings to the Tom Adams Financial Centre, liberally sprinkled with Gothic churches, cathedrals and a synagogue. North of the city along the coast is the Deep Water Harbour, where massive cruise ships dock, dominating the skyline and disgorging their cargo. Nearby, the Kensington Oval is a mecca for all cricket lovers. The site of some of the most exciting international matches, it attracts an enthusiastic and noisy crowd who cheer and jeer to a cacophony of whistles, drums and calypso. To the south of the town is Carlisle Bay, the best anchorage on the island, where yachts seek refuge from the ocean, just as they have done for centuries. Many ships have ended their lives here and it's a prime wreck diving site as well as a great beach.

Bay Street runs along Carlisle Bay to reach the Garrison Savannah, an area of major historical significance. During the colonial era the British military stationed here built grand fortresses, batteries and signal stations in addition to their domestic buildings and a prison. What was once the parade ground is now a race track, popular with early morning joggers and fitness fanatics but transformed on race days when it is packed with noisy crowds, horses, jockeys and trainers. The Barbados Museum is here, together with the Barbados Gallery of Art, the National Cannon Collection and Bush Hill House, now named George Washington House in honour of the US President who lived here briefly as a teenager.

There are several good beaches close to the capital, popular with Barbardians at weekends. Try Batts Rock Beach, Brandons, Paradise Beach, Aquatic Beach or Browne's Beach, all in the parish of St Michael.

Inland you discover the reason for Barbados' colonization by the British. Swathes of sugar cane can be found on the rolling hills and the southern flatlands – this remains the major agricultural crop. The fertile soil has produced sugar for 360 years and the landscape still reflects plantation life, founded on the backs of slaves. Narrow, twisty roads wind between the fields, snaking their way from one village to another. Grand plantation houses dot the countryside, together with signal stations on strategic high points. These were built to give warning of any slave revolt but were rendered obsolete by the telephone and are now tourist attractions. Everywhere there are lush gardens, whether they are small patches in front of a chattel house or acres of land surrounding a former mansion. Flowers grow profusely and are a gardener's dream.

West coast

The west coast, also known as the Platinum coast, is lined with luxury villas, hotels and apartments, interspersed with a few lodgings for those of more modest means. This is the place to

Totally tropical
When in Barbados... take it easy and lime with the locals at one of a hundred beachside bars.

mingle with the rich and famous and do a bit of name dropping and spotting. It is one long, but narrow, stretch of golden sand running around bays and coves and overhung with picture book coconut palms and casuarina trees for shade. All beaches are public, so you can sit on the sand at Sandy Lane and spot celebrities, or try Paynes Bay, Folkestone and Carlton, also in the parish of St James. Further north you have Mullins, Six Men's Bay and Heywoods in St Peter.

The North
The north is wild with a dramatic coastline of cliffs and caves gouged out by booming waves, exhilarating on a rough day. There are rocky coves where you can rummage around in pools or find a spot for a picnic when the weather is calmer. River Bay is a beautiful spot while Little Bay is dramatic with its cliffs and ledges. The island may not be mountainous but there are some dramatic views over the Scotland District where the coral limestone has collapsed in cliffs and gullies before falling away into the sea.

East coast

Everything changes on the east coast and the pace of life drops considerably. This deserted shore, buffeted by Atlantic winds and eroded by the ocean waves, is where surfing, hiking and beachcombing are the main attractions. Bathsheba and Tent Bay, St Joseph, are both good beaches with rocks and pools, while Martin's Bay, Consett Bay and Bath Beach are worth exploring. Clearly the fresh air and exercise has a soporific effect because there is no nightlife to speak of, but this is compensated by the fact that the most beautiful part of the island, the Scotland District, is on the east coast.

Trip planner

Any time of year is holiday time in Barbados but some months are better than others, depending on what you want to do. The climate is tropical, but rarely excessively hot because of the trade winds. Temperatures vary between 21°C and 35°C, the coolest and driest time being December to May, and a wet and hotter season from June to November. Rain is usually heavy when it comes but Barbados has rarely been hit by hurricanes. When Tropical Storm Lily struck in September 2002 around 150 houses were damaged, mostly in the Parish of St Philip, but there was no loss of life. Bajans said they hadn't seen anything like it since Hurricane Janet in 1955.

If you want a carnival atmosphere then time your visit for Crop Over in July/August, but book flights, accommodation and car hire well in advance as everything is very busy. Bajans return home from all over the world for Crop Over and the partying goes on for five weeks. Other musical events worth aiming for are the Jazz Festival in January, Holders Season in March and the Celtic Festival in May with lots of music, dance and sports.

Cricket lovers should aim to take in a Test Match or an inter-island match to see top international players at the Kensington Oval (closed for redevelopment until the end of 2006), but there are cricket festivals at other times of the year and of course matches every Sunday in villages around the island. The main event planned is the Cricket World Cup to be played in March and April 2007. Even if you know nothing about cricket a match at the Oval is worth seeing for the audience. The stands throb to the beat of drums and whistles, calypso and comedy, this is more than just the national sport, it's almost a religion.

A weekend

If you have only a weekend to spend on the island, you probably won't want to do much except relax. Take advantage of the beach with maybe a good restaurant in the evening and a bar with live music or a nightclub afterwards. If you are on the west coast, spoil yourself at the *Cliff* or *Lone Star*, then head to the *Casbah* nightclub to see who's playing. Those on the south coast should try *Josef's* or *Pisces* for romantic seafront dining and then wander down to St Lawrence Gap, the 'happening' place.

A week or more

With a week to spare, it's well worth dragging yourself away from your sunbed to explore inland and put Barbados' history as a British colony into perspective. Hop on a bus one day and have a morning's sightseeing and shopping in Bridgetown. Hire a car for part of your holiday and tour the island. You can drive all round Barbados in five hours, but temptation will get in your way and you'll stop frequently. You'll also probably get lost, as road signs are not a big feature and the island is criss-crossed with hundreds of little twisty roads through sugar plantations and villages.

A northern tour could take in Speightstown, the Animal Flower Cave, Farley Hill, the Barbados Wildlife Reserve and Grenade Hall Signal Station, St Nicholas Abbey and the Morgan Lewis Sugar Mill. A day in the middle of the island could encompass the Sir Frank Hutson Sugar Museum, Harrison's Cave, the Flower Forest, Orchid World, Gun Hill Signal Station and Sunbury Plantation House.

Another day could be spent at Bathsheba, hiking along the old railway on the coast, strolling around Andromeda Gardens or lolling about in rock pools among the boulders.

At night, you can really hit the town, with *Harbour Lights* beach party on Mondays, *Fisherman's Pub* on Wednesdays when there is a steel band, Oistins fish fry on Fridays with calypso, soca and live music, and a club at weekends. If you're a real night owl and still have energy for more, Baxters Road rumshops are open all night every night and the first bus home starts at 0500.

If you have the luxury of two weeks on Barbados why not move around a bit? Spend a few days on the west coast first, to wind down and enjoy the beach. Take a boat trip, go snorkelling with the turtles or dive one of the many wrecks from the colonial era littering the seabed. Then, when the jet lag is behind you, move to an apartment on the south coast for the nightlife around St Lawrence Gap. Finally, stay in a guesthouse on the east coast for a different view of paradise, go walking, beachcombing or take a good book and find a hammock.

Contemporary Barbados

Barbados is a relatively young country, having won its independence in 1966 after more than three centuries of British rule. The experience of being an oppressed people, both as a colony and as slaves, remains a live issue and Barbadians have struggled to find an identity and a voice.

In the 18th century, when slavery was at its peak, Africans outnumbered their British masters by three to one. Sugar provided a livelihood for everyone and Barbados was relatively quiet with few slave uprisings. This has been attributed partly to the large military and police presence and the fact that there was nowhere to hide on the small island, but also to slightly better treatment of slaves by their masters than on some other islands. However, resentment grew, particularly after the Haitian Revolution and when emancipation was being debated in England. In 1814 the slaves rose up and burned the cane fields and plantation buildings in a show of defiance – an event still celebrated today.

Slavery was finally abolished in 1838 but not much changed for the blacks. They ended up as very cheap labour and were unable to purchase land of their own. The white plantocracy remained in control of all productive land, becoming allied to a rising merchant class in Bridgetown so as to form an entrenched elite with total financial and political power. Poverty ground down the working class, whether they were black or white (known as redlegs, descended from indentured labourers and deported convicts). Tens of thousands left the country to work on the Panama Canal and those who made money and survived returned to form the nucleus of a black middle class. Resentment grew again at neglect by Britain, poor wages, poor housing and poor education, and in the 1930s there were riots. Out of conflict, the seeds of a labour movement grew, led by great Barbadians such as Grantley Adams and Errol Barrow, who went on to found the two main political parties and steer the country to independence.

Today, Barbados' political leaders are black and there is a large black middle class, but the landowning and business elites remain white. There are still extremes of poverty and wealth, but these are not nearly as noticeable as elsewhere in the Caribbean, making the social atmosphere relatively relaxed.

Just as the political landscape has changed, so there has also been a shift in the economy. Sugar is no longer king but has been deposed by tourism. Land formerly devoted to sugar cane has been sold for the construction of hotels and golf courses. This move to a service economy has been successful, bringing incomes on a par with Portugal or Greece and pushing Barbados up to 27th place in the UN Human Development Index with one of the highest literacy rates in the region. As a result, there is little resentment towards foreigners as has been found in parts of Jamaica or Trinidad. Holidaymakers go home with nothing but good things to say about the friendliness of Bajans and the excellent – if sometimes slow (this is the Caribbean after all) – service they received in hotels and restaurants.

Barbados has a population of 268,000, more than any of the Leewards or Windwards and making it one of the 'big four' in the Anglo-Caribbean community. With a population density of 1,614 per square mile it is also one of the most crowded countries in the world. Add to that over half a million stopover visitors a year and even more cruise ship passengers on day trips and you can understand the immense pressure on land.

There are currently three threads in the tapestry of Bajan society and culture. While turning its back on its colonial days, Barbados has followed the trend in the region and opened the door to a neo-colonial master. From fast food chains to programmes on the television, US culture is insidious. Young Barbadians now choose to study in the USA or Canada rather than in the UK and, if they come home at all, come back full of the ideals of North America. However, Afro-Caribbean roots are of paramount importance to most Bajans, reflected in the rhythm of home grown music and festivals such as Crop Over, as well as food derived from slave rations of staples brought over from Africa.

The third strand is a legacy from Britain. However much Bajans have grown apart from the former mother country there is one love they can not shake off: cricket. In this sport-mad country, everyone has an opinion on the latest matches, the team selection and the state of the West Indies side. In the rare event that you are stuck for a topic of conversation, you can rely on cricket to start a lively debate and a cricket match is symbolic of the way Bajans approach life – with fun, drama and huge enjoyment in the sport amid a cacophony of noise.

The island is currently undergoing a massive construction boom as Barbadians prepare for the 2007 Cricket World Cup. Hotels are being renovated and expanded, new condominium developments are springing up, roads and other infrastructure repaired and

★ **Ten of the best**

Best

1 **A day on the beach at Bottom Bay** The ultimate tropical beach – deserted, with pink sand and coconut palms, p35.

2 **Sunbury Plantation House** A fine example of how the colonial elite spent their days, p37.

3 **Friday night at Oistins for fish fry** Loads of fun, fish, music, dancing – and more fish, p42.

4 **Orchid World** Thousands of orchids in a riot of colours, p62.

5 **Hiking the old railway track on the east coast** An impressive, wild Atlantic coastline, p85.

6 **Surfing at the Bathsheba Soup Bowl** A mecca for keen surfers. Test yourself against the huge Atlantic rollers, or just sit back with a beer and watch these dudes battling with the waves, p84.

7 **A plate of flying fish and chips** The national dish fills a hole any time of day or night, p113.

8 **Crop Over Festival** The ultimate party if you've got the stamina. Parades, jump-ups and competitions, p144.

9 **Cricket on the green** Take in a Sunday afternoon village match and get tips from the knowledgeable crowd, p159.

10 **Horse racing at the Garrison** Calypso gone wild with excitement, place your bets and join in the fun, p166.

improved, while the main project – the rebuilding of the Kensington Oval cricket ground – will give Barbados a state of the art sports and concert venue to rival any in the world. Everyone is talking about it and it will affect everyone's lives. Barbados will host six matches in the Super Eight round and the Finals, for which some 30,000 fans are expected. To avoid traffic jams, schools will be closed and exams rescheduled regionally. The disruption is considered worth it for the benefits it will bring, both during the event and for the long-term impact on Barbados as a place to live and to visit.

Travel essentials

The main port of entry is the Grantley Adams International Airport on the south coast, 16 km from the capital, Bridgetown. Very few flights arrive late at night, but if you are delayed, there are hotels a short taxi ride from the airport (see p98). Cruise ships are frequently used by people wanting to stop off for a few days in Barbados (see p22) and there is a new ferry service to neighbouring islands. The easiest way of seeing the island is definitely by hiring a car, giving you flexibility and convenience. However, buses are cheap and run all over the island from Bridgetown, so with care and a bit of organization you can get around in the company of Bajans. Taxis will take you anywhere, but are relatively expensive (see p26).

Getting there

Air

From the UK and Europe All direct scheduled services are from London, with **British Airways** flying daily and **Virgin Atlantic** five or six times a week, from Gatwick. **BWIA** has three flights a week from Heathrow and **BMI** has three flights from Manchester. These flights take about eight hours. Fares vary considerably bet- ween seasons. European school holidays push up prices to £700 (Virgin) in August, with another peak in January to February, but prices as low as £264 (British Airways) can be found on the internet for October. Charter flights are variable and can not always be booked without an accommodation package, but there are companies offering regular services, see www.barbados.org/flights. From November to April there are direct weekly Sunday flights from Frankfurt with **Condor** for €550-900. **Journey Latin America**, **T** 020-87478315, www.journeylatinamerica.co.uk, can arrange flights and tours.

From North America and Canada BWIA is the main carrier, with direct flights from Atlanta, Miami, New York, Washington DC and Toronto and connecting services from other cities. Flights from Miami take about 3½ hours and 4½ hours from New York. Cheap flights can be booked on the internet and are on offer from as little as US$300 from Miami in the autumn, while from New York they range from US$400 in the autumn, US$675 in summer, to US$790 in winter. Flights from Toronto start from US$635. **Air Jamaica** flies from New York and Philadelphia, **American Airlines** from Miami and New York, **US Airways** non-stop from Philadelphia with same-day connections from 38 cities, **Delta** non-stop from Atlanta, and **Air Canada** from Montréal and Toronto. Prices more than double in high season and flights are heavily booked at Christmas and Crop Over. Not all airlines have the same dates for the beginning of high, shoulder and low seasons, so shop around, as one day can make a difference of several hundred dollars.

Airlines

Air Canada T 1-888-2472262, www.aircanada.ca
Air Jamaica T 1-800-5235585 (North America/Caribbean),
T 0208-5707999 (UK/Europe), www.airjamaica.com
American Airlines T 1-800-4337300, www.aa.com
BMI T 0870-6070222, www.flybmi.com
British Airways T 0845-7733377, www.britishairways.com
BWIA T 0870-4992942 (UK/Europe), T 1-800-5382942
(North America), T 1-868-6272942 (Caribbean/South America),
www.bwee.com
Caribbean Star T 1-800-744STAR, www.flycaribbeanstar.com
Condor T 0180-2337135 (Germany), www.condor.de
Delta T 1-800-2414141, www.delta.com
LIAT T 1-268-4805625, www.liatairline.com
US Airways T 1-800-4284322, www.usair.com
Virgin Atlantic T 01293-450150, www.virgin-atlantic.com

Caribbean connections There are dozens of daily flights to
other islands and Guyana if you want to island hop. The main
regional airlines are **LIAT**, **Caribbean Star**, **BWIA**, **Air Jamaica**
and **American Eagle** (part of American Airlines). LIAT has two
passes called Explorer tickets: the *LIAT Explorer* costs US$225 (peak
season 1 July to 31 August, 5 December to 6 January, two weeks
around Trinidad Carnival and two weeks around Easter), or US$199
(off-peak, the rest of the year), valid for 21 days, with a maximum
of four stops permitted at Tortola, Antigua, St Kitts, Nevis, St
Thomas, St Croix, Sint Maarten, Guadeloupe, Dominica, St Lucia,
Barbados, St Vincent, Grenada, San Juan and Tobago. The *LIAT
Super Explorer* costs US$425 (peak season) and US$399 (off-peak)
for a 30-day ticket, allowing unlimited stop overs in all its
Caribbean destinations except Guyana and Santo Domingo. LIAT
also operates an airpass in which each flight costs US$75, valid for

21 days, with a minimum of three stop overs at all its Caribbean destinations except Guyana and Santo Domingo. These tickets may only be issued in conjunction with an international flight to a Caribbean gateway, the itinerary must be settled in advance, with no changes permitted, and no child discounts. A return ticket with stopovers is often cheaper than the airpass. BWIA's *Caribbean Airpass* covers all its destinations including Caracas and Paramaribo, but if you want to stop anywhere west of and including Kingston, Jamaica, it will cost more. A first class unlimited mileage pass is US$750 (US$900 including Jamaica) and the economy pass is US$450 (US$550). There is also a four-day pass for US$350 (US$450), but this can only be bought in the UK, Europe, New Zealand and Australia and you have to travel to the Caribbean with BWIA. You can have any number of stop-overs, but no destination may be visited more than once, unless making a connection, and the entire journey must be fixed at the time of payment; dates may be left open. This airpass is valid for 30 days, with no refunds given for unused sectors. It may not be used between 19 December and 6 January.

Caribbean Star has an airpass, called the *Starpass*, which allows passengers up to four flights for US$299 on any of its 80 daily flights to 13 destinations in the Lesser Antilles and Guyana, including Barbados. The pass must be bought outside the Caribbean in conjunction with an international return ticket, but there are no restrictions on travel dates. It can be used with any number of stopovers and you can return to your original start point or use it as a part of an 'open jaw' ticket, returning from another island.

Airport information
The airport is modern and well equipped having been rebuilt and extended in 2004/2005. There is a BWIA/LIAT connection desk before Immigration. There is a helpful Barbados Tourism Authority office, Barbados National Bank (very slow), bureau de change (0800-2400) in the arrivals and departure areas, post office, car hire

and shops including an inbound duty free shop (very useful, saves carrying heavy bottles on the plane). Across the car park there are two lively rumshops, one of which, *Frankie's*, does good meals and snacks. The shop in the gas station is open when terminal shops are closed, selling food and newspapers. Car hire companies are to the left as you come out of customs. Taxis stop just outside customs. Check the notice board on the left as you come out of arrivals for official taxi fares. Drivers may attempt to charge more if you haven't checked; talk to the dispatcher if necessary. There is a bus stop just across the car park, with buses running along the south coast west to Bridgetown, or (over the road) east to the Crane and Sam Lord's Castle. Departure tax is US$12.50 (B$25), not payable for stays of less than 24 hours.

Sea

Star Ferries, **T** 0890-649649, www.starferries.com, began a new fast ferry service in 2005 from Barbados to St Lucia, Martinique, Dominica, Marie-Galante, Guadeloupe and St Martin, for 400 passengers and cars. Scheduled services run on Wednesday, Friday and Sunday with a maximum 40 kg baggage per person. In Barbados contact **Remac Tours Ltd**, Chapel Street, Speightstown, St Peter, **T** 4220546, www.remactours.com. Charters and one-day tours are sometimes available.

The cruise ship passenger terminal is just north of Bridgetown, with an extensive area of shops in mock chattel houses. The cruise ship passenger tax is US$8.50. **Easy Cruise**, www.easycruise.com, started cruising the islands from Barbados in the 2005/2006 winter season. Leaving Barbados on a Sunday, you arrive in St Vincent on Monday, Martinique on Tuesday, the Grenadines (Bequia) on Wednesday, Grenada on Thursday, St Lucia on Friday and back to Barbados on Saturday. You can get on and off the ship anywhere you like as long as you stay on board at least two nights. Rates vary but are as little as US$32 per cabin including port taxes but no meals. If you arrive by yacht, mooring facilities are available at the

Shallow Draft next to the Deep Water Harbour, or there are calm anchorages in Carlisle Bay (see p52). Ask at the harbour or at the Boatyard on Carlisle Bay for yacht passages to other islands.

Getting around

Bus

Buses are cheap, fun and frequent, but are also crowded. There is a flat fare of B$1.50 per journey, so if you change buses you pay again. Almost all the routes radiate out of Bridgetown, so cross-country journeys are time-consuming if you are staying at the beach. However, there are some circuits which work well; for example any south coast bus to Oistins, then cross-country College Savannah bus to the east coast, then a direct bus back to Bridgetown; any west coast bus to Speightstown, then a bus to Bathsheba on the east coast, then a direct bus back to Bridgetown. Bus stops are marked 'To City' or 'Out of City'. For the south coast ask for Silver Sands route.

Around Bridgetown, there are plenty of small yellow privately-owned minibuses with B licence plates and route taxis with ZR licence plates; elsewhere, the big blue and yellow buses (exact fare required or tokens sold at the bus terminal) belong to the **Transport Board**, **T** 4366820. Private buses tend to stick to urban areas while the public buses run half empty in rural areas and in the evening. There is a City Circle route, clockwise and anti-clockwise round the inner suburbs of Bridgetown which starts in Lower Green.

Terminals for the south: Fairchild Street for public buses, clean, modern; Probyn Street, or just across Constitution River from Fairchild Street for minibuses; further east by Constitution River for ZR vans. Terminals for the west: Lower Green for public buses; west of Post Office for minibuses; Princess Alice Highway for ZR vans, but from 1800-2400 all leave from Lower Green. During the rush hour, all these terminals are chaotic, particularly during school term. On most routes, the last bus leaves at, or soon after, midnight and the first bus leaves at 0500.

→ Travel extras

Money The currency is the Barbados dollar, which is pegged at B$2 for US$1. There are notes for B$2, 5, 10, 20, 50 and 100 and coins for B$1, 25 cents, 10 cents, 5 cents and 1 cent. Many tourist establishments quote prices in US dollars. Banks will only change the US and Canadian dollar, Euro and sterling. Credit cards are widely used.

Safety Take normal precautions against theft, which has risen in recent years. Do not leave your things unattended on the beach, shut windows and lock patio doors at night. There are some areas of Bridgetown, such as Nelson Street, you should avoid late at night. Baxters Road is generally safe although it attracts cocaine addicts (*paros*). Take care when walking along deserted beaches (avoid at night; there have been machete attacks) and watch out for pickpockets in tourist areas. If hiring a car, watch out for people who wash the vehicle unasked and then demand US$5.

Telephone The IDD code for Barbados is +246.

Vaccinations The only vaccination certificate required for entry is yellow fever if you are arriving from an infected area.

Visas Visitors from North America, Western Europe and Commonwealth African countries do not need a visa. Visitors from most other countries are granted a short stay visa on arrival, and tourist visas are not necessary. Officially, you must have a ticket back to your country of origin, as well as an onward ticket, to be allowed in. Immigration officers do check. You will also need an accommodation address on arrival. Extending your stay is possible at the Immigration Office, Careenage House, Bridgetown, T 4269912, open 0830-1630. It costs US$12.50 and is time consuming. Take your passport and return ticket.

! Errol Walton Barrow, one of Barbados' national heroes, has his picture on the B$50 note, which is popularly known as an 'Errol'.

There are two routes from the airport: Yorkshire buses go straight to Bridgetown, others go along the south coast past the hotels to Bridgetown. For a shopping trip into Bridgetown from the south or west coast hotels from Monday to Saturday, call the **Bridgetown Visitor Shuttle, T** 4312078, US$3, 0830-1600. It is of course cheaper to hop on a regular bus for US$1.50.

Car
The island is fairly small but it can take a surprisingly long time to travel as rural roads are narrow and winding. The Adams Barrow Cummins highway runs from the airport to a point between Brighton and Prospect, north of Bridgetown. This road (called the ABC, or industrial access highway) skirts the east edge of the capital, giving access by various roads into the city and to the east coast. Its roundabouts are named after eminent Bajans, including Sir Garfield Sobers, Errol Barrow and Everton Weekes. Roads into Bridgetown get jammed morning and afternoon. Drivers need a US$5 visitor's driving permit (Visitor Registration Certificate) even if you have an International Driving Licence. Car hire companies will usually sort it out for you. Mini-mokes are fun but not recommended in the rainy season. Car hire is efficient and generally reliable. A medium-sized car will cost on average US$105 per day, US$400 per week, but you can get cheaper deals with small companies. There are often discounts available (including free driver's permit) and tourist magazines frequently contain 10% discount vouchers. Petrol prices have risen sharply in line with international prices. The speed limit is 80, 60 or 40 kph depending on the type of road. Drive on the left.

Cycling
Bridgetown is not recommended for cyclists. The roads are dangerously busy, traffic moves quite fast round the one way system and the road surface is uneven and potholed. Out of town you should be careful on narrow, twisting roads, which also have potholes. There have been many accidents with bicycles and most

→ Rum tours

Foursquare Rum Factory and Heritage Park, see p37, modern distillery on the site of an old sugar factory.
Mount Gay Visitor Centre, p57, very good 45-minute tour of the blending and bottling plant, with a video, an exhibition of rum, rum tasting and shop.
West India Rum Refinery, see p58, the world's only working distillery on a beach. Tour of the rum distillery with the history of rum and rum making, followed by a spell on the sand.

people who rent bikes lose their US$150 deposit because of damage or theft, so it can work out very expensive. Besides being dangerous and expensive it is also hot work and lots of people give up after one day. Take lots of water and sun screen.

Taxi

There are plenty at the airport, the main hotels, and in Bridgetown. There are standard fares, displayed just outside 'arrivals' at the airport, and are also listed in the *Visitor* and *Sunseeker*. Between the airport and any point north of Speightstown US$27.50, to Holetown US$19, to Bridgetown Harbour US$15, to Garrison US$12, to Oistins US$8; between the city centre and Sam Lord's Castle US$19, to Oistins US$10, Dover US$9; between Sandy Lane and Oistins US$18. There are no taxi meters. Vehicles which look like route taxis but with ZM licence plates, are taxis plying for individual hire, and will charge accordingly.

Walking

The sights of central Bridgetown can be toured on foot in a morning with no difficulty. There is a good walking route along the old railway track, from Bath to Bathsheba and on to Cattlewash. See p30 for details of walking tours.

Tours

Air tours

For those who want to make a lot of noise buzzing around the island, **Bajan Helicopters**, T 4310069, www.bajan helicopters.com, offers tours from US$75 for 20 minutes (30 miles), US$125 for 30 minutes (50 miles), right round the coastline. The heliport is near the deep water harbour at Bridgetown. Also try **Barbados Light Aeroplane Club**, T 4287102 ext 4676, for a 30-minute flight, costing US$37.50.

Boat tours

There are a large number of motor and sailing boats available for charter by the week, day or for shorter periods. Large boats make you wear life vests for safety when you snorkel, the smaller ones don't. Day trips are from Shallow Draught and go up the west coast to the southern end of the marine park to snorkel over the reef then to Paynes Bay to snorkel with turtles. There is some fish feeding but only of bigger fish away from the coral. **Tall Ships Incorporated**, T 4300900, tallships@sunbeach.net, runs *Excellence I* and *Too, Irish Mist, Tiami I and II* and *Spirit of Barbados* catamarans, US$45-61.50, *Harbour Master* and *Jolly Roger* (the last two being boozy fun cruises). Other large catamarans include *Cool Runnings*, T 4360911, www.coolrunningsbarbados.com, run by Captain Robert Povey and his wife Annika, and *El Tigre*, T 4177245, www.eltigrecruises.com, who offer the usual cruises and snuba. *Heatwave*, T 4299283, www.caribbean-connection.com/heatwave, a 57-ft catamaran usually takes about 30 passengers but will go out with only 10, good lunch, friendly crew, but not particularly eco-conscious, US$61.50, also runs Wet'n'Wild cruise, a combination of cruise, snorkelling, jet skis, kayaks and banana boat rides. However, if you want something less crowded, try *Rubaiyat*, T 4359913, lunch and dinner cruises, US$65, maximum 20 people, or one of the others with names like *Small Cats*, T 4216419, smallcats@sunbeach.net, *Super Cats*, **T** 4383709, superbcats@ hotmail.com, or *Wild Cats*, **T** 4183687, smallships@ caribsurf.com, which take small groups. *Stiletto III* and *IV*, **T** 4298967, stiletto@funbarbados.com, are catamarans formerly used for racing and now owned by brothers Peter and Graham Allen for lunch, sunset or turtle cruises, unfortunately with more fish feeding and turtle feeding. Captain Ron, **T** 2623792, www.barbadossailing.com, offers private cruises on *Wasn't Me!* and *Why Not? Ocean Mist*, a 60-ft power catamaran, run by Ian and Jennifer Banfield, **T** 4367639, offers one-day charters of five to six hours, maximum 16 passengers, US$75 including food, drink and snorkelling gear, or the boat can be chartered, bareboat, for seven days to the Grenadines, maximum eight people, US$750 a day plus US$1,250 for fuel, clearances and licences. *Wayzäro*, **T** 4237196, is a glass-bottomed boat used for party cruises and snorkelling trips such as the four-hour Sunday lunch trip with steel pan, sunset cruises from 1600 including drinks. Others are moored in the Careenage in Bridgetown, with a telephone number displayed. Most are equipped for fishing and snorkelling, and will serve a good meal on board. Rates and services offered vary widely. **Caribbean Safari Tours**, at the Ship Inn, St Lawrence, **T** 4275100, offers day tours to the Grenadines and other islands, with yacht charter as an option.

Bus tours

A criticism of the tours with some companies is that it can take 1½ hours to pick up everyone from hotels and those further north do not get the full tour through Bridgetown and Holetown. **Williams Tours Ltd**, **T** 4271043, charges US$50-75 for a day tour, has a sign up in the bus: 'no 10% service charge is paid with the tour price', heavy pressure selling of tapes, limited drinks from bar. **Bajan Tours**, **T** 4372389, is cheaper and better value than some, no pressure on tipping, US$32.50 per half day, US$50 full day including lunch. Longer tours generally include lunch. The

Barbados Museum and Historical Society, T 4270201, does a Heritage Island Bus Tour which includes a tour of the museum, US$62.50 adults, children half price.

Cycling tours

Odyssey Tours, T 2280003. Offer ecological and historical excursions by bike. **Flex Bicycle Rentals**, T 2311518 (mob), 4240321, gmgriff@sunbeach.net, run by Paul Griffith, offer bike hire US$15, and run tours on Fridays and Saturdays.

Jeep tours

Island Safari, T 2925337, www.islandsafari.bb, conducts tours in 4WD Land Rovers so they can get to some less accessible beaches, US$40 per half day, US$57.50 full day with lunch, US$90 land and sea tour, kayaking and rumshop safari also on offer. **Adventure-land**, T 4183687, runs a full day tour in a yellow vehicle 0830-1500, with or without lunch, popular with cruise passengers. They also offer mini-buggy off-road driving on the east coast and hiking or snorkelling in Carlisle Bay. **Ultimate Outback Tours**, T 4205418, limbolady@sunbeach.net, offers 4WD charter with driver US$47/hour, minimum four hours, up to six passengers, children welcome, lunch at restaurant en route. **ATV Quest**, Morgan Lewis, St Andrew, T 4229213, atvquest@caribsurf.com, offers guided tours on quad bikes from the Morgan Lewis Windmill through the Scotland District and down to the beach on the east coast. A driving licence is required.

Submarine tours

To see the underwater world without getting wet, the *Atlantis Submarine*, T 4368929, www.atlantisadventures.bb, is at Shallow Draft Harbour, day and night dives at US$80, children aged four to twelve go half price, discounts in low season. The tour starts with a short video and then you go by bus to the deep water port or join the launch at the Careenage. The boat takes about 10 minutes to get to the submarine. Sit at the front to be first on the sub – an advantage as then you can see out of the driver's window as well as out of your own porthole. Two divers on underwater scooters join the submarine for the last 15 minutes, putting on a dive show. Once a week there is an evening dive at 1700 when the submarine turns on its lights. T his is the best dive as the submarine goes down to 130 ft where there is not much sunlight, but by turning on its lights you can see all the pretty colours. Booking is necessary, check in is 30 minutes before dive time and the whole tour takes 1½ hours. They also offer the *Atlantic Seatrec* (semi-submersible), US$35, and snorkel tours, US$27.50.

Taxi tours

You may have to bargain hard for tours by taxi but always agree a fare in advance. They will sometimes try to exceed the official rate per hour of US$16. On the west coast they will often charge US$25-30 per hour. **Linda Mayers**, lindamayers@hotmail.com, is recommended by the BTA and is a knowledgeable and reliable driver with a six-seater station wagon who charges US$16 per hour. For a half-day tour, expect to pay US$75 and for a full day US$125-150 depending on what you want to do.

Walking tours

The **National Trust** organizes *Hike Barbados*, three-hour Sunday walks at 0600 and either 1530 or 1730 (depending on the moon, take a torch). Details are in tourist magazines or contact **T** 4262421, www.barbados.org/hike. Their walk to Chalky Mount in the Scotland District has been recommended. Three speeds: 'stop and stare' (1530 only), five to six miles; 'here and there', eight to ten miles; and 'grin and bear', 12 to 14 miles. **Ocean Adventures**, **T** 4362088, www.oceanadventures.bb,

The National Trust

The National Trust runs an **Open House** programme of visits to interesting private houses on Wednesday afternoons from January to April every year (B$15, children 5-12 half price, B$6 for members of foreign National Trusts (see below). **Boyces Garage** do a tour plus entrance for B$35, T 4251103. The houses are not necessarily old, in fact many of them are modern in the extreme, often occupied by diplomats. A National Trust Heritage passport is available for sites maintained by the Trust. A full passport costs US$35 and gives a 50% discount to 15 National Trust sites as well as invitations to the open house programme. A mini passport costs US$18 and allows half price entry to five sites. The Duke of Edinburgh Award Scheme (Bridge House, Cavans Lane, Bridgetown, T 4369763) and National Trust joint scheme also arrange early Sunday morning walks to places of historical and natural interest, see Walking tours, p30. There is a reciprocal free entry to National Trust Properties for members of the National Trust in the UK, Australia, New Zealand, Fiji and Zimbabwe. The same arrangement applies to members of the National Trust for Historic Preservation in the USA and the Heritage Canada Foundation. The National Trust Headquarters is at Wildey House, Wildey, T 4369033, natrust@sunbeach.net, open 0800-1600. It houses the Trust's collection of antique furniture and the Euchard Fitzpatrick and Edward Stoute photography collections.

offers a four-hour walk through the rainforest ending at a cave. Be prepared to get wet and muddy and wear sturdy shoes. The Tourism Authority provides a useful, free leaflet with map for a self-guided walking tour of Bridgetown.

Tourist information

The **Barbados Tourism Authority** (BTA) has its main office in Harbour Rd, Bridgetown, **T** 4272623, www.barbados.org, open Monday-Friday 0900-1700. There are also offices at the deepwater harbour, **T** 4261718 and the airport, **T** 4280937. Two good sources of information are *Visitor* and *Sunseeker*, published fortnightly and distributed for free by Barbados's two daily newspapers. *Sunseeker* has an amazing listing of every possible club and society, down to Progressive Ballroom Dance and Clay Pigeon Shooting. If you want to meet fellow Soroptimists, Rehabilitation Therapists, Astronomers or Girl Guides...there you go. It also lists where to worship, entertainment and daily events. *Signature* is a free, glossy magazine with articles on culture, profiles, environment, business etc. *Sporting Barbados*, www.sportingbarbados.com, is another free glossy, plenty of useful information. *Ins and Outs of Barbados*, www.insand outsofbarbados.com, also free, is published annually, a glossy with lots of historical articles as well as advertising and a useful year-round calendar.

Maps

Ordnance Survey Tourist Maps include Barbados in the series, 1:50,000 scale with inset of Bridgetown 1:10,000, available from the Public Buildings in Bridgetown, the museum, airport and from some bookstores in town. GeoCenter publish a Holiday Map, 1:60,000 scale with inset of Bridgetown, 1:7,500, the Garrison, the west coast and the south coast with sites of tourist interest marked. Esso distributes a road map with the free *Barbados in a Nutshell* booklet (advertising), with insets of Bridgetown, the west coast and the south coast with hotels marked. The Tourism Authority does a useful, free leaflet with map for a self-guided walking tour of Bridgetown.

South coast 35 This is where the fun starts. The island's airport is here, along with the best beaches, a plethora of hotels, restaurants and bars, and plenty to do day and night.

Bridgetown and around 46 The island's capital is not the automatic choice for a base but is well worth a visit, especially the historic Garrison Savannah.

West coast 62 The 'Platinum Coast', as it's known, is a favourite with the jet setting rich and famous but its Caribbean, palm-lined beaches are also accessible to lesser mortals.

The North 76 The unspoiled north coast presents a very different side to Barbados – a combination of storm-battered cliffs and rocky coves. Inland, the Scotland District is one of the island's most beautiful parts.

East coast 83 The wild and untamed east coast offers other attractions such as hiking and horse riding and is especially popular with surfers.

South coast

Kick off your shoes, put on your swimsuit and head for the sand. The south coast caters for the package holiday end of the market, with lots of mid-range, mid-quality hotels packed in along the western end in districts with the charming English names of Hastings, Worthing and Dover. The advantage of the south coast is that it is close to the airport and has the better beaches, with wider expanses of sand and gently sloping entry to the sea. It is popular with a younger crowd and there is lots of night-time action. Families with young children and teenagers find plenty to do by day and by night, and it is easy to get around the island for excursions when you've had enough of sun, sea and sand.

▸▸ *See Sleeping p98, Eating and drinking p114 and Bars and clubs p129.*

East of the airport

The southeast coast is less built up than the southwest and boasts some of the island's finest beaches, especially Bottom Bay, though the Crane is a magnet for lovers of Sunday brunch and steel bands. Away from the beach, Sunbury Plantation House gives a real insight into the history of Barbados.

◉ Sights

★ Bottom Bay
From Six Cross Roads (Six Roads since a roundabout was installed to sort out traffic accidents) take Highway 5 heading northeast. After the turning for Sam Lord's Castle look out for a small signpost on a telegraph pole for Bottom Bay. Go down a small road through grazing cattle to the parking place near Bottom Bay House. Map 4, F8, p220

This just has to be the most beautiful beach in Barbados and one of the best in the Caribbean. What is more, it is often deserted, even in high season. Steep cliffs surround the small bay and the sand is a glorious pale coral pink. Walk down the steps carved between the cliffs onto a huge expanse of sand, where a clump of palm trees grows in true holiday brochure fashion. Sometimes there is a boy on the beach who will offer to climb up to get coconuts down for you to drink the cool milk. He will ask for an extortionate tip for his labour, but the coconuts are free. There are no facilities as such but there is a little hut under the coconut palms where you can sometimes hire sunbeds. The only shade is under the palm trees or the cliffs, but with few other people around, that is usually plenty. The sea can be rough with quite big waves, and is better for jumping and splashing about than serious swimming. Before you leave, go up on top of the cliffs to look back down onto the beach, then walk round to get a good view of the next bay south, Cove Bay, with the ruins of Harrismith plantation house overlooking the water.

Sam Lord's Castle

From Six Roads roundabout take Highway 5 and follow signs.
Map 4, G7, p221

Sam Lord's Castle is the site of an all-inclusive hotel, now closed and in receivership. Sam Lord reputedly hung lanterns in the trees to look like the mouth of Carlisle Harbour (see p52) and lure ships onto Cobbler's Reef where they were shipwrecked. There is supposed to be a tunnel from the beach to the castle's cellars to facilitate his operation. The proceeds made him a wealthy man although the castle was probably financed from his marriage to an heiress who later left him and fled to England. Another legend has it that the captain of one of the wrecked ships murdered Sam Lord in London in 1844. The castle is not particularly old or castle-like, being in fact a regency building dating from 1820.

Foursquare Rum Factory and Heritage Park

Foursquare, St Philip, Highway 6, **T** 4201977. *US$6, children US$3. Mon-Fri 0900-1700, Sat 1300-1800, Sun 1100-1700. Tours every 30 mins. Rum punch and miniature included. Map 4, H4, p221*

The new distillery makes ESA Field White Rum and also specializes in spiced rum. It is the most modern rum distillery in the world on the site of an old sugar factory. The Heritage Park comprises the old sugar buildings, with sugar machinery, craft market, pottery, bottling plant, folk museum, pet farm, pony stables and Foundry Art Gallery.

★ Sunbury Plantation House

T 4236270, www.barbadosgreathouse.com. *Daily 0930-1630. US$7.50, or US$20 including lunch in the courtyard restaurant (5-course formal dinner in the house costs US$93).Turn north at Six Roads roundabout, the plantation house is at the first T-junction. Map 4, G3, p221*

One of the oldest houses on the island and a fascinating insight into plantation life, Sunbury (pronounced Sun-berry) was built around 1660 by the Chapman family. They were among the first settlers and related to the Earl of Carlisle (see p190), who granted them land. Chapmans are mentioned on the first map of the island in 1638 and again in Richard Ford's map of 1674 which shows a cattle mill on the Chapman plantation. It changed hands and names several times and it was the Barrow family who named it Sunbury after their home in England. One of the Barrow heirs was Colonel in Charge during the Easter Rebellion of 1816 (see p44 and p191), during which the plantation suffered damage valued at £4,000. The slave revolt at Sunbury was led by a friend of Bussa called King William, who was later put to death. The estate never really recovered and in 1835 John Barrow sold up and emigrated to Newfoundland. The house was bought by sugar magnates, the

Daniels, then, in the late 19th century, by a Scots emigrant, Alistair Cameron. Two of his daughters remained living at Sunbury until their deaths in 1980 and 1981, when the land was sold to the estate manager and the house was sold to Angela and Keith Melville. They took on a house which had been untouched for 100 years, and although they lived in it for a few years, in 1984 they moved back to their previous house and opened up the whole of Sunbury House as a museum. In 1995 a fire swept through the upper floors destroying the old timbers, wooden floors and antiques, except for those in the cellar. Substantial renovation was needed but the massive walls and a few floorboards were intact. The house/museum is now crammed with a very busy collection of mahogany furniture, art, china and antiques found elsewhere on the island or returned to Barbados from abroad. You can roam all over it as, unusually, there is access to the upstairs rooms. In the cellars, you can see the domestic quarters with a good collection of old optical instruments and household items. In the cellar and in the garden there are lots of carts and gigs, including one donated by Sir Harry Llewellyn, the British Olympic showjumper of the 1950s and 1960s.

Crane Beach

Take Highway 5 from Six Roads and follow signs for The Crane Hotel. You can either park by the hotel and pay a fee to walk through the grounds, or carry on to a little roundabout by Crane House and turn down a narrow lane which leads to steps giving access to the northern end of the beach for free. Parking is not good here and extremely difficult on a Sunday. You may have to reverse out.
Map 4, H6, p221

Another fabulously deep beach with plenty of powder soft coral pink sand, while the water is picture-book turquoise. The waves

! There was once a crane on the top of the cliffs at this beach
● for loading and unloading ships, hence the name.

To be young and to be alive in Barbados tonight,
I feel as if I were in paradise already.

Errol Walton Barrow,
on the birth of a new Caribbean nation,
November 30, 1966.

are a bit rough for swimming but very popular with body surfers and great for splashing about and generally having fun. The Crane Hotel is perched on top of cliffs at the southern end of the beach. The cliffs provide natural shade if you don't want to hire an umbrella. A rickety path winds part of the way around the cliffs, a useful vantage point from which boys drop fishing lines into the water, but the sea has eroded the rocks so that the cliff now overhangs the waves and the end of the path has collapsed.

Sunday is the popular day here, when the Crane Hotel lays on a breakfast buffet with Gospel singers (1000-1130, US$20 including VAT), followed by a huge buffet lunch (1230-1500, US$25 plus drinks) to the accompaniment of steel pan. They will even hire you clothes so you can look decent when you come off the beach to eat in the restaurant, which has an eagle's eye view of the bay. The hotel opened in 1867, making it the oldest hotel on the island, although the original building dates from the 18th century. The more recent construction of timeshare apartments mars the skyline but they are invisible from the beach. There are sunbeds and umbrellas for hire on the beach for B$10 each and some watersports equipment such as boogie boards at B$10 per hour or B$20 per day.

Foul Bay
Just south of Crane Beach, take turning signed 'Public Access to Foul Bay Beach'. Map 4, I6, p221

Despite the unappealing name, Foul Bay is another long stretch of idyllic pink sand with turquoise water. It is wide and open and less crowded than at the Crane although conditions in the sea are similar. This is the longest beach on this coast, with large cliffs at each end. There are no facilities but there is some shade and a few picnic tables and benches. A small fishing fleet comes ashore here and you can sometimes see turtles just beyond the waves.

West of the airport

There is little to distinguish the places west of the airport nowadays as the coast is entirely built up from Hastings to Oistins, but St Lawrence Gap is the place to go for nightlife and Maxwell is the base for the Barbados Windsurfing Club. St Lawrence Gap, known as just The Gap, has recently been titivated with a boardwalk along the water, new street lighting, better parking and general beautification works. Tucked away behind the hotel strip is the Graeme Hall Nature Sanctuary, where you can go for a change of scenery and a bit of birdwatching, while the fishing village of Oistins sparks into life on Friday nights for a fish fry. The south coast is great for windsurfing and kitesurfing, particularly to the east of South Point, where Silver Sands is a windsurfer's mecca, but watch out for rip tides if you are swimming. This part of the coast lies within the parish of Christ Church.

◉ Sights

Miami Beach

Off Highway 7, just east of Oistins. *Map 3, J8, p219*

Also known as Enterprise, busy Miami Beach is divided in two parts, calm or rougher, so it's suitable for small children or older, braver types. Swimming is good, but it's not safe to go out beyond your depth, hence the presence of a lifeguard. Windsurfing is popular, particularly for those at an intermediate level. There is lots of shade under casuarina and broadleaf trees and everything you could need for a pleasant day on the beach. Catamaran tour parties often anchor here for lunch if the west coast is too rough for them to go up to see the turtles at Alleynes Bay. Facilities include beach chairs and umbrellas for rent, parking, a toilet block, a drinks and snacks van and picnic tables.

★ Oistins

Highway 7. *Map 3, J8, p219*

Oistins, the main town in the parish of Christ Church, was named after Edward Oistine, a plantation owner in the area. It was important in colonial times as one of the sites where Roundheads and Cavaliers clashed, with the Royalists achieving a stand-off for six months. On 11 January 1652 a meeting took place in Ye Mermaid Tavern in Oistins, when the Articles of Agreement were signed. This later became known as the Charter of Barbados when recognized by the Commonwealth Parliament.

Christ Church Parish Church overlooks the town and is notable for its cemetery containing the **Chase Vault**. When the vault was opened in 1812 for the burial of Colonel Thomas Chase, the lead coffins were found scattered around inside. It happened again in 1816, 1817, 1819 and 1820, whereupon the coffins were removed and buried separately in the churchyard. Whatever had been moving them around had thrown them about with such violence that one coffin had taken a chunk out of the vault wall.

Oistins is now the main **fishing port** with colourful boats pulled up on the shore and you can still see fishermen mending and making nets. The **fish market** is worth visiting, even if you don't want to buy, to see the expert skill and lightning speed with which the women fillet flying fish and bag them up for sale. Flying fish being the signature dish of Barbados, they make it into something special here, celebrating every Friday night with a fish fry around the market. Dozens of wooden stalls are opened for the occasion and the smell of well-seasoned fried fish wafts along the coast attracting hundreds of hungry people keen to fill up before hitting the bars and night spots of the south coast. Oistins is also the venue for an Easter **Fish Festival**, see p146, celebrating fishermen's skills with demonstrations of fish boning, boat racing and crab racing, helped along with steel pan music and dancing.

★ **Best**

Beaches

Ocean Park

Balls Complex, Christ Church, **T** 4207405, www.oceanpark
barbados.com. *Daily 0900-1800, US$17.50, children US$10.*
Map 3, I9, p219

Just inland from Oistins, this new attraction has been added to a
mini golf course (US$20, children US$12.50 for both the park and
mini golf). Several aquariums and pools recreate ecosystems such
as mangroves, rocky coast and coral reef. There is a rather
inhospitable ray pool with half a dozen southern stingrays and
other fish and a tunnel where you can see sharks and reef life
swimming over and around you. The best exhibits are indoors in
small tanks where you can see the symbiosis of anemones and
shrimp, for example. The complex is still very new and more time
and work is needed before it is worth the entrance fee.

Dover Beach

St Lawrence Gap. *Map 3, J6, p219*

This beautiful horseshoe shaped bay with pristine white sand and
turquoise water is the stuff of dreams. It's a great place for lazing
around, sunbathing and cooling off in the sea, which is usually
calm and protected. There are windsurfers and other watersports
for hire.

The Easter Rebellion

The 1816 Easter Rebellion was an uprising by slaves who thought (incorrectly) that William Wilberforce had introduced a bill in the British parliament granting slaves their freedom. It was thought by the slaves that the Barbados plantation owners were denying them this freedom. Despite destroying a large acreage of cane fields, no owners or their families were killed and the uprising was quickly crushed by the West Indian Regiment. Several hundred slaves were killed in battle or hanged afterwards, including the best-known leader, an African called Bussa, and Washington Francklyn, a free man of mixed race who was thought, probably erroneously, to have planned the rebellion. Some 123 slaves were exiled to Sierra Leone.

Sandy Beach

Worthing. *Park at the Carib Beach Bar.*
Map 3, J5, p219

The curve of the coastline and an offshore reef has produced a lovely beach with shallow, calm water, almost in a lagoon, making it ideal for families with small children. Also known as Carib Beach, it's a good place to learn to windsurf because of the lack of waves and there are beach chairs, umbrellas and towels for hire. The Carib Beach Bar attracts all sorts and is lively during the day and at night. It is particularly popular on Sunday nights when Bajans pack the place for eating, drinking and dancing.

Graeme Hall Swamp

Worthing, Highway 7, **T** 4359727, www.graemehall.com.
0800-1800. Map 3, I6, p219

The largest expanse of inland water in Barbados, Graeme Hall Swamp, near St Lawrence Gap, has 36 acres of wetland and mangroves around a lake. It is a natural habitat for birds and there are 18 resident species and 150 migrants. Some 180 bird species have been recorded in Barbados, mostly migrants and mainly shore birds and waders, which breed in North America and winter in South America. The first to pass through are normally sighted in July when they flock into the swamp. A boardwalk, ponds and visitor facilities are open to the public but the rest is to be a bird sanctuary for scientific research only. Three endangered Caribbean duck species are found here and there are also more familiar flamingoes and parrots around the ponds. The swamp was saved from development by a retired Canadian, Peter Allard, who bought it in 1994.

Accra Beach
Rockley, off Highway 7. *Map 3, J5, p219*

In the middle of the hotel strip, this beach is understandably popular and often crowded. Strong swimmers should head out to a small, man-made reef of huge boulders for the best snorkelling on the south coast. Sunk in the late 1990s, it is already growing coral and is home to large schools of blue tang, jacks and other colourful fish. A young hawksbill turtle sometimes hangs around there and you may be lucky enough to see him if not too many boatloads of snorkellers have been there first. You must be careful on such a young reef not to damage anything by standing on it or poking around with your hands as coral dies if you touch it. Depending on the waves, Accra Beach is also good for bodysurfing or, alternatively, just sitting watching the fit types performing and strutting their stuff. Facilities include a car park, kiosks for vendors and boogie boards and beach chairs for rent. There's also a lifeguard.

Bridgetown and around

The capital, Bridgetown, on the southwest corner of the island is small but busy and full of life. Once called Indian Bridge, after the basic bridge across the Careenage, it was later called the Town of St Michael, after the parish in which it lies. It is set around Carlisle Bay, with the Deep Water Harbour for cruise and cargo ships to the north and in the middle, an inlet known as the Careenage, at the mouth of Constitution River, where schooners and other trading vessels used to tie up. It got its name because the schooners were careened onto their sides so that the hulls could be cleaned or mended. Nowadays small craft such as sport fishing boats tout their wares to visitors, overlooked by restaurants with a dominant nautical theme. The southern part of the bay is beach, with watersports and nightlife on offer, popular with a young crowd.

▶▶ *See Eating and drinking p117 and Bars and clubs p131.*

Downtown Bridgetown

Aside from the historic area at Garrison, this is the most interesting part of Bridgetown, with National Heroes Square as the city's hub and the Careenage a reminder of its nautical past. There are no really large buildings except Tom Adams Financial Centre, which houses the central bank and the Frank Collymore Concert Hall, see p139. Swan Street is now a lively pedestrian street where Barbadians do their shopping and street music is sometimes performed. On Broad Street, previously called Cheapside, Exchange Street and New England Street, you will find a whole range of sophisticated shops catering for tourists, with large shopping malls, duty-free shops and department stores. More developments are planned along by the Careenage where old warehouses are being converted for other uses.

Sights

National Heroes Square
Map 5, E8, p223

This small, triangular 'square' is the hub of central Bridgetown. It was called Trafalgar Square until 1999 and there is a statue of Lord Nelson, sculpted by Sir Richard Westmacott and predating its London equivalent by 30 years. Admiral Nelson visited Barbados with his fleet in 1805, a few months before his death, and the square was named in 1806, with the statue being erected in 1813. The name has recently been the subject of some controversy as it was thought to link Barbados too closely with its colonial past. After more than 30 years of independence, the Little England jibes were a trifle past their sell by date. Nelson was turned 180° so that he no longer looked down Broad Street, the main shopping area. He is to be moved when a suitable home can be found and when someone can work out how to do it. Moving something that heavy is no mean feat. The square is now celebrating 10 official national heroes, including Sir Grantley Adams. There is a memorial to the Barbadian war dead and the fountain commemorates the piping of water to Bridgetown in 1861.

Parliament Buildings
Map 5, E8, p223

To the north of the National Heroes Square are the neo-Gothic Parliament Buildings. The West Building was built in 1871 and the East Building was finished in 1874. They are imposing grey buildings with a red roof and green shutters. The clock tower on the west wing dates from 1886, the original having been demolished, and now houses public offices. The East Building, housing the Senate and the House of Assembly, has stained glass windows depicting British kings and queens from James I to Queen Victoria and even includes Oliver Cromwell. You can walk between the buildings.

Constitution River
Map 5, E8/9, p223

Running south from National Heroes Square is **Chamberlain Bridge**, for centuries one of the capital's two main wooden bridges over Constitution River. It was given its present name at the beginning of the 20th century in honour of Joseph Chamberlain, British Colonial Secretary, who gave the island a large chunk of money in grants and loans to keep the economy afloat. In 2005 it was demolished when bits started falling off it and is to be rebuilt using modern materials. The second bridge, going off southeast from the square, is the **Charles Duncan O'Neal Bridge**, named after one of the founding fathers of democracy in Barbados (1879-1936) and a national hero. The old bridge was pulled down in 1967 and replaced with a wider, stronger, modern structure to take the increased volume of vehicular traffic. If you are driving, the junctions can be a bit scary until you get the hang of the one-way system as locals drive very fast over the river. The market and one of the bus stations create extra hazards on the south side of the bridge.

St Michael's Cathedral
St Michael's Row. *For services, see p187. Map 5, D10, p223*

Take the northeast exit out of National Heroes Square along St Michael's Row to reach this 18th-century Anglican cathedral. It has a fine set of inscriptions and a single-hand clock. The first building was consecrated in 1665 but destroyed by a hurricane in 1780. The present cathedral is long and broad with a balcony. It has a fine vaulted ceiling, at one time the widest in the world, and some tombs (1675) have been built into the porch. Completed in 1789 with £10,000 raised in a lottery, it became a cathedral in 1825 with the arrival of Bishop Coleridge, but suffered hurricane damage in 1831.

● *Sir Grantley Adams and his son, Tom Adams, both prime ministers, are buried here along with other famous Barbadians.*

▶ Jewish settlement

By the 1680s there were 300 Jews in Barbados – 5% of the total population – and by the middle of the 18th century there were 800. They were heavily involved in the sugar industry, advancing capital and credit or owning plantations. The Morgan Stanley Mill was Jewish and their influence was so great that Swan Street was once known as Jew Street. However, life was not a bed of roses for all of them. Jews were taxed more heavily than other residents and regularly expected to present the Governor with a 'Jew Pie', gold coins baked in a pie crust. They were not allowed to trade with blacks and were classed as 'foreigners and strangers'. In 1831 a storm destroyed the synagogue and the congregation began to decline, with emigration brought on by the end of slavery and the drop in the price of sugar. Enough Jews remained to rebuild the synagogue but by the turn of the century only about 20 remained. In 1929 when only one man, Edmund Baeza, acknowledged his Jewish heritage, the synagogue was sold and in the 1950s was the office of the Barbados Turf Club. A small revival in the 1930s was brought about by the arrival in 1932 of a few Polish Jews fleeing Europe en route to Venezuela. They started working as peddlers and gradually attracted friends and other family members. Now there are Polish, Romanian, American, German, Guatemalan, Cuban and Chinese (converts) Jews and numbers fluctuate between 50 and 80.

Queen's Park
Map 5, A12, p223

If you continue east, you reach Queen's Park, a pleasant, restful park just outside the city centre, with the largest tree in Barbados:

a baobab with a circumference of 61½ ft (18 m), thought to be over 1,000 years old. Queen's Park House was once the residence of the General commanding the British troops in the West Indies. It was known as King's House until Queen Victoria came to the throne, but is now a small theatre (Daphne Joseph-Hackett Theatre, see p139) and art gallery. There is a small restaurant and bar, which does a good lunch and a buffet on Friday.

Nidhe Israel Synagogue
Synagogue La, **T** 4277611. *Mon-Fri, 0900-1200, 1300-1600. Map 5, C7, p223*

The synagogue is an early 19th-century building on the site of the 17th-century original, one of the two earliest in the Western hemisphere. The original synagogue was built in the 1660s by Jews fleeing Recife, Brazil, who heard that Oliver Cromwell had granted freedom of worship for Jews and gained permission to settle in Barbados. Cromwell granted the first pass to settle in 1655 to Dr Abraham de Mercado, an elder of the Recife society and his son David Rafael. Jews in Barbados were granted the right to worship publicly even before Jews in London, and Barbados was the first British possession to grant Jews full political rights at the beginning of the 19th century. Recently painstakingly restored, the synagogue is now used for religious services again and is open to visitors.

● *The tomb of Benjamin Massiah, the famous circumciser of 1782 lies on the left hand side of the graveyard, just inside the entrance.*

Public Library and Law Courts
James St and Coleridge St. *Map 5, A7, p223*

In a block along Coleridge Street are the Public Library, founded by Scots philanthropist Andrew Carnegie, the Law Courts and the Central Police Station. At one time the Legislature, the Law Courts and the jail were on this site, leading Henry Nelson Coleridge to write in 1832: "His Majesty's Council, the General Assembly, the Judge, the juries, the debtors and the felons, all live together in the same house".

● *On the other side of the road opposite the library, is the Montefiore fountain, now dry. It was built as a drinking water fountain in 1864 by John Montefiore in memory of his father, a leading merchant who died of cholera.*

Government House
St Michael. *Map 3, H4, p219*

First known as Pilgrim House, it was purchased for the Government in 1736 from John Pilgrim, a Quaker, as the permanent residence of the Governor. It is a typical example of a plantation Great House, with arched porticoes, jalousie window shutters, verandas, a parapet roof and a circular driveway, as well as delightful gardens. It is not open to the public, however, except for special functions and National Trust open days (see p31).

St Patrick's Cathedral
Bay St, at the corner of Jemmotts La, St Michael, **T** 4262325. *Map 5, H12, p223*

This is the Roman Catholic cathedral, started in 1840 but not long built before it was gutted by fire in 1897. The current building dates from 1899 and was built through subscriptions and donations from the Government and, Protestants and Jews as well as Catholics. It became a cathedral in 1970.

! A Barbadian planter, Sir John Colleton, asked King Charles II of England for land in America. He was granted an area known today as the Carolinas and founded the settlement of Charleston, named after the king. Many others followed him. In fact, most of the early Governors were Barbadians.

Carlisle Bay

Bay St. *Map 5, H8, p223*

Bay Street runs south of the city centre hugging the edge of Carlisle Bay, which is a surprisingly good beach considering how close it is to town. Yachts anchor here, snorkelling and diving parties call in, and there are beach facilities: umbrellas, sunbeds, food, drink and parking at the Boatyard. Hugely popular are the water trampoline and the inflatable water slide which looks like an iceberg. It's a lively place and often packed with cruise ship visitors. A marine reserve is being created here with a series of six interlocking underwater marine trails. There are four shallow wrecks and more are to be added in an area of 160,000 sq m. One of the wrecks is the *Cornwallis*, which was torpedoed in 1942 by a German U boat; the hull was moved from deeper water in Carlisle Bay into the shallower Marine Reserve.

Garrison Savannah

South of central Bridgetown is the Garrison area on the strategic southeast point guarding the entrance to Carlisle Bay and the capital. In the face of a possible French invasion in 1785, a permanent garrison was built as the headquarters of the British army in the region. The 64-acre site adjacent to Charles Fort and St Ann's Fort is now the Garrison Historic Area. Surrounding the parade ground, now the six-furlong race course, are numerous 17th- to 19th-century military buildings constructed from brick brought as ballast on ships from England. They are built on traditional British colonial lines, examples of which can be seen throughout the Caribbean and in India. Painted bright colours, some now contain government offices. There are several memorials around the oval race course. In the southwest corner is one commemorating the 'awful' hurricane which killed 14 men and one married woman and caused the destruction of the barracks and hospital on 18 August 1831, and outside the Barbados Museum in the northeast corner there's another to the men of the Royal York Rangers who fell in action against the French in Martinique, Les Saintes and Guadeloupe in the 1809-10 campaign. The Savannah, now a race course, is used at other times for early morning or evening jogging, exercising the horses, informal rugby and basketball games and there's usually something going on on Sunday afternoons. Later, at night, it's taken over by prostitutes.

◉ Sights

Fort Charles
Needham Point. *Turn south at the Pepsi plant.* Map 6, E1, p224

Fort Charles was the largest of the many forts which guarded the south and west coasts. It forms part of the gardens of the Hilton Hotel which has been rebuilt. Only the ramparts remain but there are a number of 24 pounder cannons dating from 1824. The Mobil oil refinery was the site of the naval dockyard. Built in 1805, it was subsequently moved to English Harbour, Antigua. The buildings were then used as barracks before being destroyed in the 1831 hurricane. The military cemetery was the burial ground for the Garrison and the headstones make interesting reading. It appears, for instance, that disease claimed more lives than military action.

! After the French Revolution the threat of an invasion by France grew stronger. To increase their manpower, the British Army started to recruit black slaves. They were made free men and paid a wage, which attracted thousands to the Black Corps. By 1799 the corps became the West Indian Regiment, creating a formidable fighting force of 15,000 men.

Garrison Savannah, St Ann's Fort and military buildings
Garrison Secretary, **T** 4260982. *Map 6, E5, p224*

St Ann's Fort is still used by the Barbados defence force. You cannot
enter but look for the crenellated signal tower with its flag pole on
top. It formed the high command of a chain of signal posts, the most
complete of which is at Gun Hill (see p59). The long, thin building is
the old drill hall. The Main Guard, overlooking the savannah, has a
nice old clock tower and a fine wide veranda. It has been turned into
an information centre and houses exhibits about the West Indian
Regiment. It is also a good place from where to watch the horse
racing. Outside is the National Cannon Collection, an impressive
array of about 30 cannon, some of which are mounted on metal
'garrison' gun carriages (replaced with wooden ones during action
as they were prone to shatter). There are also a number of newer
howitzers, dating from 1878. Major Mike Hartland, who collected
many of the cannon on display, conducts tours. Contact the **Tall
Ships Garrison Historic Tours**, **T** 4300900.

Barbados Museum
T 4270201, www.barbmuse.org.bb. *Mon-Sat 0900-1700, Sun
1400-1800. US$5.75, children US$2.90. Library available for research
purposes. Mon-Fri 0900-1300. US$10 plus VAT. Map 6, A8, p224*

The Barbados Museum is housed in the old military prison on
the northeast corner of the savannah. Based on a collection left by
Reverend NB Watson (late of St Lucy Parish), it is well set out through
a series of 10 galleries. It displays natural history, local history, a fine
map gallery including the earliest map of Barbados by Richard Ligon
(1657), colonial furniture (Plantation House Rooms), military history
(including a reconstruction of a prisoner's cell), prints and paintings
which depict social life in the West Indies, decorative and domestic
arts (17th- to 19th-century glass, china and silver), Africa and its

people in the Caribbean, a children's gallery and one to house temporary exhibits. The museum shop has a selection of craft items, books, prints and cards.

George Washington House
Bush Hill, **T** 2285461. *Map 6, B5, p224*

George Washington House, or Bush Hill House, is where the future first president of the USA stayed in 1751 for a few months when, as a 19-year old, he accompanied his sick brother Lawrence (who later died) to search for a cure for his brother's TB. This was George Washington's only excursion outside his homeland and Bridgetown was the largest town he had seen. At that time, Barbados was a more advanced society than that of America, with better health care. Washington was introduced to the delights of the theatre as well as banquets and fine dining, where he met the leading scientists, engineers and military strategists of the day. He contracted smallpox but the skill of an English doctor saved him. As a result of his brush with death, he acquired immunity to the virus which enabled him to survive an outbreak of the disease during the American War of Independence which killed many of his men. The house has been beautifully restored but is not currently open to the public.

Mallalieu Motor Collection
Pavilion Court, Hastings Rd (Highway 7) **T** 4264640. *Daily, US$5. Map 6, E7, p224*

Bill Mallalieu has opened his collection of vintage cars to the public. The collection boasts a Bentley, Daimler, Humber, Vanden Plas Princess, Wolseley, Lanchester and many others. The old cars are often used in processions such as the Holetown Festival, escorting Miss Holetown and other personalities.

Around Bridgetown

The suburbs of the capital sprawl along the south and west coasts and quite a long way inland. Many of the suburban areas are very pleasant, full of flowering trees and 19th-century coral stone gingerbread villas. Further inland, in the very heart of the island, are two of the best sights: Gun Hill Station and Orchid World.

◉ Sights

Harry Bayley Observatory

Clapham, St Michael, not far from Banks Brewery (see below), **T** 4245593. *Fri 2030-2330. US$4, children US$2.50. Map 3, H5, p219*

The observatory is operated by the Barbados Astronomical Society, which opens it to the public once a week. It is the only observatory in the Anglo-Caribbean and is a chance for northern visitors to look through a 14-inch reflector telescope at the Southern Hemisphere stars and planets, which aren't all visible from North America and Europe.

Banks Brewery

Wildey, **T** 2286486, www.banksbeer.com. *Tours Mon-Fri 1000, 1200 and 1400. US$6, children 10-15 US$3, no children under 10. Tour packages including transport from anywhere on the island, US$16. Map 3, H5, p219*

The beer is brewed and bottled here and there is a small museum: Brewseum, beer garden and gift shop. In the museum you can see how the beer used to be brewed in copper kettles. Nowadays it is a computer-automated facility with stainless steel vessels.

▶ Tales of the rich and infamous

Stede Bonnet was an unlikely pirate, having been born into a prosperous planter family in Barbados. He became a major in the island militia, a magistrate and plantation owner, and was never short of a bob or two particularly after his advantageous marriage to a local heiress. However, for some unexplained reason he jacked the whole lot in, bought a sloop with 10 guns, recruited a pirate crew of 70 and set off for the High Seas. A series of colourful escapades brought him international renown and a brief partnership with the fearsome Edward Teach, also known as Blackbeard. His downfall came after several raids along the New England coast. Two warships were sent to capture him and bring him to justice. The 'pirate of good position' was later hanged, but went down in history as the only pirate to have bought his own ship.

Mount Gay Visitor Centre

Brandons, St Michael, near the deep water port in Bridgetown on the Spring Garden Highway, **T** 4258757, www.mountgay.com. *45-min tours every 30 mins Mon-Fri 0900-1545. US$6, children free, or a special luncheon tour Tue and Thu US$27.50. Map 3, G2, p219*

Mount Gay claims to be the world's oldest rum distiller and offers a very good tour of the blending and bottling plant, with a video, an exhibition of rum, rum tasting and shop. Excellent rum cocktails at the bar. For details of the Mount Gay Distillery, see p79.

Tyrol Cot

St Michael, **T** 4242074. *Mon-Fri 0900-1700. US$5.75, children US$2.90. Map 3, F4, p218*

Built in 1854 by William Farnum, this house is preserved for posterity by the National Trust for being the home, from 1929, of Sir Grantley Adams, the founder of the Barbados Labour Party, Prime Minister of the short-lived West Indies Federation and of the newly independent Barbados. It was also the birthplace of his son, Tom Adams, who was Prime Minister in 1976-85. The house is built of coral stone and ballast bricks and is furnished with mahogany pieces. There is a Heritage Village with craftsmen at work, plus a chattel-house museum, gardens and a restaurant in the old stables.

West India Rum Refinery and Malibu Beach Club

Brighton, Black Rock, St Michael, **T** 4259393. *Mon-Fri 0900-1700 with the last tour at 1545. US$7.50 for tour, US$27.50 tour with lunch, also US$37.50 day pass to Malibu Beach Club. Free shuttle from hotel. Map 3, F2, p219*

Just north of the town centre are Brandons Beach and Brighton Beach, the latter being home to the *Malibu Beach Club* attached to the West Indies Rum Distillery. The distillery produces Malibu, a rum and coconut mix which is, surprisingly, one of the fastest growing spirits in the world. Less well known is the Malibu Lime, a blend of white rum and lime which is only available in Barbados and France. There are guided tours of the distillery but you can also opt for a day on the beach, taking advantage of the watersports on offer. Beach chairs, umbrellas and changing facilities are available on any package, but if you go for the lunch pass or day pass you receive a voucher for US$5 off the non-motorized watersports package with transport to and from your hotel. If you take the half-hour tour you get a complimentary Malibu and mix on the beach, while the lunch tour grants you four free drinks with your barbecue and the special day pass a whopping ten free drinks. Book a day in advance as the package is very popular with cruise ship visitors.

St George's Parish Church
St George. *Map 3, E6, p218*

One of the oldest churches on the island, it was one of only four parish churches to escape damage during the 1831 hurricane. Inside there is a magnificent altar painting of the Resurrection by Benjamin West, the first American president of the Royal Academy, and there are statues and other sculpture, including work by Richard Westmacott, the creator of the statue of Lord Nelson in National Heroes Square, Bridgetown.

Gun Hill Signal Station
St George, **T** 4291358. *Mon-Sat 0900-1700. US$5 (children half price), guide book US$1. Map 3, D7, p218*

The signal station has its origins in the slave uprising of 1816, when it was decided that a military presence would be maintained outside Bridgetown in case of further slave uprisings. It was also intended for advance warning of attack from the sea and has a commanding view of the whole of the south coast across to Bridgetown harbour. The chain of six signal stations on the island was intended to give very rapid communications with the rest of the island but was soon superseded by the telephone. The hexagonal tower had two small barrack rooms attached and would have been surrounded by a pallisade. The signal stations quickly lost importance as military installations but provided useful information about shipping movements. Gun Hill has been fully restored and there are now lots of royal connections, with visits from Prince Edward, Princess Margaret and Princess Alexandra all commemorated in photos.

! Look out for the *Nigel Benn Aunty Bar* on a bend in the road in Shorey Village. Nigel Benn, one-time UK boxing champ turned TV celebrity has a Bajan father and his aunt runs this rumshop.

Bim volumes

In addition to being called Little England, Barbados is frequently referred to affectionately as 'Bim' or 'Bimshire'. In the 1960s the musical of Barbados, Ballad for Bimshire, was staged in New York, with lyrics by Irving Burgie, who also wrote the words for the Barbados National Anthem. The Barbados Museum houses a permanent exhibition on Amerindian life called 'In Search of Bim'. Austin Clarke, winner of the Canadian 2002 Giller Prize, set his novel, The Polished Hoe, in the post-colonial West Indian island of Bimshire. The literary magazine, Bim, launched numerous Bajan and West Indian authors under its most influential editor, Frank Collymore. There's even an internet chat room for Bajans called Club Bimshire.

Prince Edward planted a tree in 1987 and came back to check on it in 1992. Informative guides will explain the workings of the signal station and point out interesting features of the surrounding countryside. The approach to the station is by Fusilier road and you will pass the Lion carved by British soldiers in 1868. The road was built by Royal Scot Fusiliers between September 1862 and February 1863 when they were stationed at Gun Hill to avoid yellow fever. The fusiliers' cookhouse has been converted into a snack bar serving food such as chicken and rice (US$5-7). There's also a gift shop.

Drax Hall
St George. *Map 4, E1, p220*

In the 1640's Drax Hall was the first place on Barbados where sugar was cultivated and the 878-acre plantation is the only estate to have remained in the hands of the same family since the 17th century. It is open only occasionally under the National Trust Open House programme, see p31.

Horses for courses
The island has moved on from the times of British colonial rule but some traditions still linger on.

★ Orchid World

Groves, St George, **T** 4330306. *0900-1700. US$7, children US$3.50. Combined ticket with Flower Forest US$11.50. Map 3, C7, p218*

Some 20,000 orchids from all over the world are grown in this 6½-acre orchid garden in a beautiful, mind-blowing display. Some are grown in the full sun, others trained on wire fences so their roots don't touch the ground, some are grown on trees, some in the ground, some in coconut shells and some in 'houses' for partial shade under nets. A path meanders down the hillside, initially through woodland, where orchids and other plants grow in their natural environment. Then you come out onto lawns where the path is directed between living fences of orchids, before you are bombarded with visual splendour in the orchid houses. The colours are breathtaking. Words cannot describe the range and variety, each one seeming better than anything seen before. Surprisingly, there are no orchids for sale, although the *Best of Barbados* gift shop will sell you orchids on tea towels, trays, mugs and numerous other souvenirs. There is also a snack bar and toilets.

West coast

Known as the Platinum Coast with luxury hotels and villas along the seafront, the west is not just for posh pensioners and well-heeled celebrities, although it has acquired that image. Low key elegance is the order of the day and standards are very high. Good quality accommodation at the cheaper end of the market can also be found if you take time to look and are prepared to walk a few minutes to the beach. Most of the west coast is a golden sand beach, although not as broad as the beaches on the south coast. Access can be tricky where there is solid development between the road and the sea, but look out for footpaths between hotels where you can get down to the water without tackling an officious hotel doorman. All beaches are public, but some hotels and restaurants block you out by cramming the narrow strip of sand with their sun beds or denying access through their property. The beaches are narrow, particularly in areas with greatest erosion, but the sea is usually calmer than elsewhere around the island. Beach erosion is a problem and a swell can wash up lots of broken coral, making it unpleasant underfoot.

▶ *See Sleeping p103, Eating and drinking p119 and Bars and clubs p133.*

Bridgetown to Holetown

The road north of Bridgetown on Highway 1 is wall-to-wall low-rise, intimate hotels and villas, punctuated by some excellent places to eat. Highway 2a runs parallel inland and goes through the sugar cane heartland, giving access to tourist sights on this side of the island.

◉ Sights

Paradise Beach
About half a mile north of the roundabout where Highway 1 begins, take a sharp left. Drive down to Batts Rock Beach, with access via a track next to Calabaza restaurant, park under the trees, then walk south to get to Paradise Beach. Map 3, E2, p218

Work on a new Sandals Resort at Paradise Beach has thankfully been shelved because they were not allowed a private beach. Meanwhile, with no hotel, the beach is beautifully deserted and there are even some old sunbeds left behind. Swimming and snorkelling is good at both Batts Rock, popular with families at weekends, and Paradise Beach. You can keep going south along the shoreline as far as Deepwater Harbour. It's a nice walk and mostly along the beach.
Batts Rock has a car park, trees for shade, a children's playground, picnic tables, shower and changing facilities, but no snack bar. Snorkelling is good here but the current can occasionally be strong.

Paynes Bay

There is access to the beach at several points but parking is limited. Try the roadside just south of Sandy Lane where the trees give shade and a path leads down to the beach; otherwise park a bit further south and walk through the Blue Monkey restaurant. Map 3, C1, p218

For the west coast, this is quite a wide sweep of pale golden sand with trees at one end and crystal clear water for swimming. Surfboards and other watersports can be arranged, and snorkelling is good here as the reef is quite close to the shore. Villas and condos line the beach and there is a restaurant/bar, slightly over-priced, where you can get refreshments and use their showers and toilets.

Sandy Lane Hotel

Parish of St James, **T** 4442000, www.sandylane.com. *Map 3, B2, p218 See also Sleeping p104*

First opened in 1961, Sandy Lane is an institution in Barbados. It has always been known for attracting a wealthy clientele and its name is synonymous with luxury. You can't miss it as you drive up Highway 1, through the gracious avenue of ancient trees, passing its grand entrance on the seaside of the road and the golf course on the inland side. Countless film stars, politicians and dignitaries have stayed here in the past and it had built up a huge list of repeat guests fleeing winter in the Northern Hemisphere for a spot of pampering in the tropical sunshine, but everything has changed since it was rebuilt at the turn of the century. The old aficionados have decamped to other hotels such as the *Coral Reef Club* or *Villa Nova*, while a number of travel journalists were banned for what they said about the place, but occupancy is now high nonetheless. Golf has always been a big thing at Sandy Lane, and it runs three golf courses with its own desalination plant for watering the greens and fairways and keeping the five man-made lakes full. The old nine-hole course dates from 1961 and the two new 18-hole courses have been designed by Tom

Fazio – Country Club and Green Monkey – built on former sugar cane land and an old quarry. Look out for the real green monkeys which live in the trees and gullies. If you can't afford to stay here, it is worth going to the *L'Acajou* French restaurant or *Bajan Blue* for the Sunday brunch buffet just to see the place but you have to book ahead to get past the gate.

● *Tiger Woods chose the 19th hole of the Green Monkey golf course at Sandy Lane as the venue for his wedding in 2004 to Elin Nordegren, of Sweden. Woods rented the entire 112-room Sandy Lane Hotel for several days for his guests, who included Bill Gates, Michael Jordan and Oprah Winfrey.*

Holetown and around

Holetown today is a thoroughly modern town but it was the place where the earliest settlers landed on 17 February 1627. The Holetown monument commemorates Captain John Powell claiming the island for England and the first landing of Englishmen from the Olive Blossom in July 1605. A secondary plaque marks the 350th anniversary of the first permanent settlement in 1627. Initially named Jamestown, it was renamed Holetown because of a tidal hole near the beach. It was quite heavily defended until after the Napoleonic Wars, though little trace of the forts can now be seen.

◉ Sights

Town centre
Map 3, B1, p218

There is a small shopping centre on the main road, with a supermarket, internet kiosk, bank and other services. Opposite is the police station, post office and a small museum (which is not always open due to staff shortages). There's access to the beach between the police station and the *Sunswept Hotel*. Here the sand is swept every morning while the early risers are jogging or walking their dogs and the *Surfside* beach bar is open for drinks, all day breakfast, snacks and full meals. Holetown is overloaded with restaurants and bistros and even with a two-week stay here you'd be pushed to try them all. Most of them are along 1st Street and 2nd Street, and both are convenient to stroll along and see what takes your fancy. Just south of the shopping centre is the **Chattel Village**, a group of replica traditional chattel houses, all brightly painted, containing boutiques, a gourmet food shop, a paper shop and a café. South again is **Sunset Crest**, another shopping area with a small fruit and veg market, an excellent internet café and banks. During the Holetown Festival in February, see p143, the roadside along this stretch of Highway 1 is crammed with people attracted by an open-air market for arts and crafts, helped along with tempting local food and drink, while the road itself is a parade ground.

St James Church
North end of town, over the bridge on the left.   *Sun services 0730, 0900. Daily 0800-1800.   Map 3, A1, p218*

Originally built of wood in 1628, the church was replaced by a light coral stone structure in 1680 which was then extended 20 ft west in 1874 when columns and arches were added and the nave roof raised. You can see the original baptismal font (1684) under the belfry and in the north porch is the original bell (1696). Many of the original settlers are buried here (although the oldest tombstone of William Balston who died in 1659 is in the Barbados Museum). Church documents dating to 1693 have been moved to the Department of Archives. There are several photos of registers, with many deaths attributed to the smallpox epidemic of 1695-1696. There is a lovely stained glass window depicting the Ascension, which was dedicated in 1924 in memory of the fallen in the First World War and paid for with public donations of B$400. The church

> **The Hag**
>
> Among the folk legends of Barbados, handed down through generations of slaves, is one about evil spirits called 'hags', similar to witches. These were women, often those in authority such as planters' wives, who were believed to shed their skin at night and turn into a ball of fire in their search for blood. If the skin was found and rubbed with pepper and salt, the hag would not be able to put it back on and would die. The last person in Barbados thought to have been a hag died in the 1920s.

was beautifully restored between 1983-1986 and the organ was restored in 2005. On the front pew is a plaque to the President of the USA and Mrs Reagan, who worshipped here on Easter Sunday, 11 April 1982.

Folkestone Park and Marine Reserve

On the beach behind the church. Museum, **T** 4222314. *Park, museum and shop daily 0900-1700. Museum B$1.15; ticket from adjacent shop. Map 3, A2, p218*

What is now Folkestone was once part of Porter's Plantation, owned for several generations by the Alleyne family, who were stalwart members of the plantocracy and political elite. The 18th century Folkestone House was marked on the 1825 Barrallier map and was built for the Alleyne family. The name celebrates the marriage in 1751 of Rebecca Alleyne (born 1725) to the Honourable William Bouverie, second Lord Folkestone, and was previously known as Church Point House.

! When the first Portuguese explorers landed they were struck by the number of bearded fig trees on the island and named it 'Os Barbados', the bearded ones.

The **Marine Reserve** stretches for 2 km from Coral Reef to Sandy Lane Hotel, including Dottin's Reef and Vauxhall Reef, but here at Folkestone Park you can snorkel in a large area enclosed by buoys. The reef is not in pristine condition but it is surprisingly rewarding as there are quite a lot of fish and you may see turtles. The hawksbill turtle frequently nests on local beaches from July to October, while leatherbacks are occasionally found nesting from February to June. Catamaran tours come up from Bridgetown for snorkelling sessions with the turtles just north of here at Alleynes Bay and to the south of Paynes Bay. The beach is not great at Folkestone but it is always crowded with people taking advantage of safe swimming and snorkelling in the cordoned off sea. Weekends are busy with families bringing enormous picnics and barbecues, cheerfully setting up home around the picnic benches under the trees. There is a lifeguard and the usual vendors and hair braiders, but no hassling. Equipment is for hire Monday to Saturday 0900-1700: sunbeds US$5; life jackets US$3; snorkelling equipment US$10 and dive/snorkelling flags are US$3. There are also glass bottomed boats to take you over the reef to two small wrecks further down the coast (US$10). A diving platform about 100 m offshore allows you to snorkel over the wrecks. There are lockers for B$2, toilets and a shower, all of limited efficiency. The **museum** is tiny, but a guide will take you upstairs in the main building to show you some dusty exhibits, with shells and fish in jars, a video of marine life along the US seaboard (not Barbados), then let you into the museum itself. There could be a lot more on underwater life – the whole thing looks tired and underfunded.

Sir Frank Hutson Sugar Machinery Museum

Inland beside the Portvale Sugar Factory off Highway 2a, north of Lawrence Johnson roundabout and St Thomas Parish Church, . **T** 4320100. *Mon-Sat 0900-1700. US$7.50 when factory is running Feb-May, otherwise US$4, children half price. Map 3, A3, p218*

The museum is in the old buildings beside the factory and is one of those special places which looks unprepossessing but is a treasure trove if you delve into it. Sir Frank Hutson amassed this large collection of machinery and the National Trust now administers it. The exhibition, on the story of sugar and its products, is fascinating for anyone interested in the history of Barbados but a guided tour is recommended. The curator is tremendously informative and there's nothing he doesn't know on the subject. Jars of excellent molasses and sugar syrup are for sale, scrumptious on pancakes or ice cream and highly recommended. During the cane-grinding season you can visit the factory to see sugar being produced.

Welchman Hall Gully

Highway 2, directly east of Holetown, St Thomas, **T** 4386671. *Daily, 0900-1700. US$6, children US$3. Map 3, A5, p218*

This is a fascinating walk through one of the deep ravines so characteristic of this part of Barbados. You are at the edge of the limestone cap which covers most of the island to a depth of about 300 ft. Maintained by the National Trust, a good path leads for about half a mile through six sections, each with a slightly different theme. The first section has a devil tree, a stand of bamboo and a judas tree. The next section goes through jungle, lots of creepers, the 'pop-a-gun' tree and bearded fig clinging to the cliff (note the stalactites and stalagmites), and then through a section devoted to palms and ferns finally the path leads to open areas with tall leafy mahogany trees, rock balsam and mango trees. At the end of the walk are ponds with lots of frogs and toads. Best of all though is the wonderful view to the coast. On the left are some steps leading to a gazebo, at the same level as the tops of the cabbage palms. Look out for monkeys at dawn and dusk. There's a small car park opposite the entrance (despite the sign to the contrary).

Harrison's Cave

Highway 2, St Thomas, close to Welchman Hall Gully, **T** 4386640. *Daily 0830-1630. US$12.50, children US$5. The bus from Bridgetown to Chalky Mount stops near Harrison's Cave and the Flower Forest. Map 2, L6, p217*

This little tourist trap has a Visitors' Centre with a snack bar, a shop and a small display of local geology and Amerindian artefacts. You are sometimes first shown an interesting video of Barbados' geology, then taken into the limestone cave on an electric 'train'. The visit takes about 20 minutes and you will see some superbly lit stalactites and stalagmites, waterfalls and large underground lakes. There is a guide to point out the interesting formations and two stops for photo-opportunities. The caves drip all the time, so expect to get wet. If you take Highway 2 heading to Bridgetown you will pass **Jack-in-the-Box Gully**, part of the same complex of Welchman Hall Gully and Harrison's Cave. **Coles Cave** – an 'undeveloped' cave nearby, which can easily be explored with a waterproof torch or flashlight – lies at its north end.

Mullins Bay

Map 2, H1, p217

Highway 1 runs up the coast to Mullins Bay, a lovely stretch of beach just south of Speightstown. There are watersports and a picnic area at the south end and the upmarket *Suga Suga* restaurant, see p121, at the north end. There's lots of activity, usually calm water and safe area for snorkelling and swimming. The restaurant hires out sunbeds (B$5) and umbrellas (B$5) for a relaxing day on the beach. There is also a basic beach bar just south of *Suga Suga*, where you can get cheaper drinks.

Life's a beach
The island's south and west coasts are lined by mile upon mile of golden sands.

Pukka chukker

The Empire's finest colonial traditions were alive and kicking. The ladies wore their crisp cotton dresses and high heels, the gentlemen were in neatly pressed shirts and Bermuda shorts. Tea in bone china cups and cucumber sandwiches were available in the clubhouse. The band struck up and everybody stood smartly to attention as they played the British national anthem in honour of the visiting team, followed by the Barbados national anthem for the home side. A moment's silence was observed in memory of a recently departed long-serving member of the club, followed by a prayer for good sport. The horses fidgeted impatiently, but finally they were allowed to start the game, which was fast and furious. The commentator's patter was informative, interspersed with comments about the backside of one of the competitors, Lucy, the only woman on a horse, playing for Cheshire, the British side. The polo ponies charged up and down, wheeling around on a sixpence and setting off in the opposite direction at a touch from their riders. The home side, the Brigands, took an early lead, but Cheshire hung on to push for a nail-biting end to the match. There are over 40 players and nearly 200 polo ponies on the island. At least 75 of them were at Holders that evening, with an almost equivalent number of young, black, stable hands to care for them, hosing them down after their exertions and preparing the next ones to do battle. A jolly time was had by ex-pats and white Bajans during and after the match. The bar did brisk business and after the ladies of the club had served tea, they turned their hands to a barbeque in honour of the visiting team and their families on holiday in Barbados. A major social event in Little England, polo remains the sport of the affluent elite, wherever it is played, and a spectacle for visitors and outsiders.

Speightstown and around

Speightstown, in the parish of St Peter, is the second largest town on the island, the major shopping destination and has the bus terminus for the north. In reality however, it's barely more than a village. It is a lively place during opening hours, but dead as a doornail the rest of the time. Pronounced Spikestown – or Spikestong in broad dialect – it is named after William Speight, a merchant and member of the Governor Hawley's first House of Assembly. An important port in the early days, when it was known as Little Bristol, because of its trade with Bristol, England, it also traded heavily with Bridgetown, 1½-hours sailing time to the south, and used to have four jetties. It once had three forts, which are no longer in evidence, while outside town were Dover Fort and Heywoods Battery. They didn't see a lot of action but the town was once invaded by Oliver Cromwell's forces when Barbados remained loyal to King Charles I. Colonel Alleyne led the Roundheads ashore in December 1651 only to be shot dead by Royalists. His forces captured the town, their only victory, and a peace treaty was later signed at Oistins.

Sights

Town centre
Map 2, G1, p217

Speightstown has several interesting old buildings and many two-storey shops with Georgian balconies and overhanging galleries. Sadly, many have been knocked down by passing lorries and a fire in 1941 destroyed almost everything near the bridge on the main road, Queen Street. On Queen Street is **Arlington**, a 17th-century single house (a single room wide). It tapers towards the back and the ground floor room was once believed to have been a chandlers, as the original owners, the Skinners, owned one of the jetties. There is a separate entrance to the first floor room and above

> ### Monkeys and medicine

The Barbados Primate Research Centre at the Wildlife Reserve not only helps farmers to control numbers of green monkeys, which are a pest and destroy crops, it also provides monkeys to zoos overseas and to laboratories for research. Many monkeys end up with pharmaceutical companies or medical research labs. Green monkey cells are used to manufacture the Sabin Polio Vaccine; one green monkey can provide up to 2½ million doses and the Primate Research Centre is responsible for 70% of the world's polio vaccine.

that there is an attic with gabled windows. **St Peter's Parish Church** was first built of timber in 1629, but it was rebuilt in 1665 and then again in 1837 in early Georgian style. However, a fire in 1980 damaged the original east window, pulpit and font. It was restored in 1983 using the original walls. On the other side of the road beside the sea is a new fish market, alongside a bandstand, used for outdoor events. The **jetty** was built in 1998 and if you walk to the end you get a tremendous view along the coast from the Arawak cement plant in the north, Port St Charles marina, the town and beaches to the south, with lovely changing colours of turquoise, dark aquamarine and purple (depending on the lenses in your sunglasses). *The Fisherman's Pub*, alongside the jetty, also has a great view of the sea and is a useful watering hole during a tour of the island (see p125), and there are diverse eating places, from a vegetarian takeaway lunchtime restaurant to the rather special *Mango's*, for which you need a reservation, see p120.

Arbib Nature and Heritage Trail
Reservations, **T** 4262421. *Walks Wed, Thu and Sat 0900-1430. US$7.50. Map 2, G1, p217*

The National Trust runs these walks (of 5½ km or 7½ km) which start from St Peter's church in Speightstown. The Arbib Trail won the annual Caribbean Ecotourism award in 1999, for the way in which it links the natural world with cultural history, and it is well worth doing. Young, local guides take small groups of hikers, exploring side streets, cricket pitches, sugar plantations, forests and beaches. Older residents of the area have provided background information, with tales of the town's history, to spice up the guides' patter.

North of Speightstown
Map 2, A1-G1, p216

North of Speightstown the coast is quieter and less developed, with fishing villages rather than holiday resorts. The road north passes through the fishing villages of **Six Men's Bay**, **Little Good Harbour** and **Half Moon Fort**, where boat building is still done on the seashore. Fishing has always been an important activity in this area and Speightstown was even a whaling station until 1903. Just north of Speightstown, at Heywoods Beach, is a new US$60-million glitzy marina called **Port St Charles**, www.portstcharles.com. It is a huge development with a massive wall around the outside to deter casual visitors, but is now an official port of entry into Barbados with coastguard, police and immigration on site for entry by yacht or helicopter. There are 145 residential units each with their own jetty, a restaurant open to the public, a yacht club, a heliport and watersports as well as capacity for six mega-yachts and 140 yachts. Water taxis chug around the lagoon taking residents to the various facilities on site or on shopping trips further afield in Speightstown. Most of the apartments and villas have already been sold, with prices ranging from US$0.7 million to US$3 million; some are available for short term holiday rental. Public access to the beach is between the marina and the Almond Beach Village, with a small road and parking.

The North

The north of the island in the parish of St Lucy is mercifully free of buildings and unspoilt (apart from Arawak Cement Plant) although new home building is increasing. It is at first green and lush around Stroud Point but becomes more desolate as you approach North Point. The northwest coast, being slightly sheltered from the Atlantic swells, has many sandy coves such as Archers Bay. The cliffs are quiet and easy to walk and you may spot turtles swimming in the sea. North Point, however, is a different story. Huge waves crash into eight miles of cliffs, creating tunnels, caves, platforms and enormous jacuzzis.

North Point to Pico Teneriffe

The sea here can be rough and wild, the waves apparently unaware that Barbados is in their way, blocking their path across the Atlantic Ocean. Round the tip on the eastern side there are some lovely coves. Some are picnic spots but many are deserted. Swimming is unsafe.

◉ Sights

Animal Flower Cave
North Point, St Lucy. *Daily 0900-1600. US$5, children US$2.50. Map 2, A3, p216*

This is one of the many caverns created by the pounding waves of the Atlantic Ocean, with its mouth above the sea when it is calm. The 'animals' are sea anemones but there are now so few of them the cave should be renamed. There are various 'shapes' in the rock

! Pico Teneriffe was named by sailors who thought it looked like the mountain on Teneriffe in the Canaries.

which are pointed out to you and a pool at the mouth of the cave where you can swim looking out to sea. The view from North Point over the cliffs and ledges is dramatic and well worth the trip even if (or particularly when) the cave is shut because of high seas. Note that the floor of the cave is very stony and can be slippery. There is a bar, toilets and souvenir shops outside.

River Bay
Map 2, B4, p216

River Bay is a pretty, sandy cove between cliffs, where a small river runs out to sea. There are facilities here and it is a popular picnic spot, but a large sign warns you not to swim because of strong currents. Good walks along the cliffs can be enjoyed, for instance from River Bay to Little Bay along the Antilles Flat, but beware as there is no shade and there are shooting parties during the season.

Little Bay
Map 2, C5, p216

From the coast several back roads go through the attractive communities of **Spring Garden** and **St Clements**. Then at **Pie Corner** you can rejoin the coast for Little Bay, which is particularly impressive during the winter months with the swell breaking over the coral outcrops and lots of blowholes. People do get in the water in the sandy bay, but you can't do much swimming if it is rough. Note the completely circular hole on the north edge of the bay. If you climb through this natural archway in the cliff, there is a big, calm pool, just deep enough to swim between the cliffs, and a line of rock on which the enormous waves break and send up a wall of spray. Wear shoes to stop your feet getting cut to pieces on the sharp rock. This is only recommended for athletic types who like to live on the edge as it involves negotiating the rocks along the cliff in rough water.

Barbados' barmy army

Barbados is an island and you would expect it to have a navy. It does, but it's a navy that never goes to sea. Barbados is the only country to have a 'landship' movement. Founded in the 1860s by a retired seaman, Moses Wood, and his friends, it was an attempt to recreate the camaraderie that Bajan sailors missed when they returned to their native land after working all their lives afloat. The fleet is commanded by an Admiral and has incorporated all the ratings of the British Navy. The crew of the Barbados Landship (Her Majesty's Landship before Independence) wears navy-style uniforms and uses the language of 'Jack Tars'. The landship attends church services, parades and festivals such as Crop Over with their corps of drum (a tuk band). Dancers make up the outline of a ship and each has a special role to play, with the admiral on the bridge, sailors scrubbing the decks and the tuk band as the engine. Their marching/dancing parodies the parades of real navies with names like 'the Changing of the Guard', 'Admiral's Inspection' and 'Rough Seas' – certainly the navy with the best sense of rhythm in the world.

Paul's Point
Map 2, D6, p216

Paul's Point is a popular picnic area and very scenic. You get a good view of Gay's Cove below (look for turtles bobbing up and down in the waves), with its shingle beach (safe for swimming in the pools at low tide) and beyond it the 240-ft high Pico Teneriffe on top of a steeply sloping cliff. The white cliffs are oceanic rocks consisting of myriad tiny white shells or microscopic sea creatures. The whole of the coast to Bathsheba is visible and it is easy to see the erosion taking place in Corben's Bay. Indeed you get an excellent impression of the Scotland District, see below, where the coral limestone has been eroded. The whole of this coast between North and Ragged Points has been zoned, no further development will be allowed along the seafront.

● *If the ground looks wet park at the millwall by the Cove Stud Farm as it is easy to get bogged down. Follow the track on foot and take the grassy path after the first house, then follow the coast in a clockwise direction, returning to the millwall across a field where cows graze.*

Inland

The northeastern part of the country is known as the Scotland District for its rugged appearance and similarities perceived by the first colonizers. But though the landscape doesn't match the majesty of the Scottish Highlands it has its own charms and there are some fascinating places to explore.

◉ Sights

Mount Gay Rum Distillery
North of the road between the St Lucy Church junction and Alexandra. *Closed to the public but tours will be restarted after upgrading works.* Map 2, D3, p216 See also p57

Although most equipment is new, the distillery has been making rum since the 19th century and produces 500,000 gallons a year. The rum is aged in bourbon whiskey barrels elsewhere and then shipped to Brandons where it is blended and bottled. The distillery is best visited during the cane cutting season when it is operating at full stretch, but is still interesting out of season when the equipment is

! All Bajan rum distilleries buy their barrels from Kentucky, ● where they have been used once for Bourbon.

cleaned ready for the new cane. If you visit the Sir Frank Hutson Sugar Machinery Museum at the Portvale Sugar Factory, see p68, the Mount Gay Visitor Centre, see p57, and this distillery, you will know all there is to know about the making of sugar and rum.

Farley Hill House
Highway 2, St Peter, **T** 4223555. *Daily 0830-1800. US$1.75 per vehicle. Map 2, F4, p216*

This 19th-century fire-damaged plantation house is an atmospheric ruin on the other side of the road from the Wildlife Reserve. It is set in a pleasant park opened by the Queen in 1966, with spectacular views over the Scotland District, right down to the lighthouse on Ragged Point. Benches have been set at strategic points so you can just sit and gaze into the deep blue yonder and enjoy the breeze coming in off the Atlantic. There is a large number of imported and native tree species, some labelled, planted over 30 acres of woodland. There are picnic benches under the trees and it is popular with Bajan families on Sundays. You are recommended to go with a seriously good picnic if you are planning to join them. It is also the venue for the annual Jazz Festival in January and was once used as the location for the film, *Island in the Sun*. From Farley Hill it is possible to walk more or less along the top of the island as far as Mount Hillaby, through woods and then canefields. However, it helps to know where you are going as the paths have a mind of their own and losing them can be uncomfortable. You will see plenty of monkeys on the way and good views.

Grenade Hall Forest and Signal Station and Barbados Wildlife Reserve
Highway 2, St Andrew, **T** 4228826. *Daily 1000-1700. US$11.50, children half price. There are buses from Bridgetown, Holetown, Speightstown or Bathsheba. Map 2, F5, p216 See also Kids, p177*

This complex of attractions has something for all the family: animals, history and nature, and it can easily absorb half a day during a tour of the north. The **Barbados Wildlife Reserve**, established with Canadian help in 1985, is set in four acres of mature mahogany off Highway 2. Most of the animals are not caged, so you are warned to be careful as you wander around the paths through the trees.

An early 19th-century **signal station** is next to Grenade Hall Forest. It was one of six erected at strategic points on the island to relay messages from Bridgetown to the north in a matter of minutes by using flags or semaphores, but it closed in 1884, rendered obsolete by the telephone. It has now been restored and an audio tape gives the history with sound effects. There are a few archaeological exhibits and photos of the rebuilding work in 1991-93. The wonderful panoramic view gives you a good idea of its original role in the communications network.

St Nicholas Abbey
Cherry Tree Hill, St Peter. *Mon-Fri 1000-1600. US$7.50, but check whether still open to the public. Map 2, E5, p216*

Approached down a long and impressive avenue of mahogany trees, and dating from around 1650, St Nicholas Abbey is one of the oldest domestic buildings in the English-speaking Americas (Drax Hall, see p60, is probably older). Three storeyed, it has a façade with three ogee-shaped gables. It was never actually a real abbey and some have supposed that the 'St' and 'Abbey' were added to impress as there are lots of 'Halls' in the south of the island. It is thought to have been built by Colonel Benjamin Beringer, but was sold to Sir John Yeamans, who set out from Speightstown in 1663 to colonize South Carolina. It is full of antiques, including an 1810 Coalport dinner service and a collection of early Wedgwood portrait medallions. Visitors are given an interesting tour of the ground floor and a fascinating film show in the stables behind the 400-year-old sand box tree. Narrated by Stephen Cave, the present owner and son of

★ **Bloomin' marvellous gardens**

Best

- Orchid World, p62
- St Nicholas Abbey, p81
- Andromeda Gardens, p86
- Flower Forest, p91

the film maker, it shows life on a sugar plantation in the 1930s. You will see the millwall in action and the many skilled workers from wheel wrights to coopers who made the plantation work, and see the importance of wind to the industry. If the windmill stopped the whole harvest came to a halt as the cane which had been cut would quickly dry out if it was not crushed straight away. The waste was used to fuel the boilers just as it is today in sugar factories.

● *From Cherry Tree Hill there are glorious views over the Scotland District.*

Morgan Lewis Sugar Mill

St Peter, **T** 4227429. *Mon-Sat, 0900-1700. US$5, children US$2.50. Map 2, F6, p216*

At the bottom of the steep Cherry Tree Hill you come to the National Trust-owned Morgan Lewis Mill, a millwall (tower of a windmill used in sugar grinding) with original machinery which the National Trust restored over a period of four years and which is now on a working farm. Built around 1776 by Dutchmen, it is the largest, complete windmill in the Caribbean, with its wheel house and sails in perfect working order. After completion of the renovation works it started to grind cane again in 1999 after a gap of 54 years. You can climb to the top of it. Note the 100-ft tail which enabled the operators to position the mill to maximize the effect of the wind.

● *On the flat savannah at the bottom of the hill is a cricket pitch, which is a pleasant place to watch the game at weekends.*

East coast

Wild and windy, unspoilt and untamed, the Atlantic Coast has a raw energy and is stunningly beautiful. Craggy cliffs form a backdrop for huge bays filled with boulders which appear to have rolled down the hillsides into the foaming surf. This is not the place for safe swimming – as Bajans say "the sea ain't got no back door" – but it is the nearest place to heaven for surfers, who can be seen out there at any time of day waiting for the right wave. Hiking is also excellent, particularly along the abandoned railway track which hugs the coastline, and other outdoor activities such as horse riding or cycling. Bathsheba is the main village, where accommodation can be found, but otherwise the east coast is sparsely inhabited and dotted with colourful chattel houses enjoying breezy sea views.

▸▸ *See Sleeping p108, Eating and drinking p126*

East Coast Road

The five-mile East Coast Road, opened by Queen Elizabeth II on 15 February 1966, runs from Belleplaine, where the railway ended, skirts Walker's Savannah and runs south to Long Pond, through Cattlewash, so named because Bajans brought their animals here to wash them in the sea, down to Bathsheba and on to Codrington College. The road affords fine views of meadows and palm trees tumbling into the ocean. Look out for grazing black-bellied sheep which are commonly mistaken for goats. There are several decent beach bars on the east coast at Barclays Park, Belleplaine, Bath and Ragged Point.

Sights

Barclays Park
Benab, North of Bathsheba, St Andrew, **T** 4229213 (beach bar). *Bus from Bathsheba or Speightstown. Map 2, H8, p217*

Barclays Park is a large open space and a good place to stop for a picnic under the shady casuarina trees. The 50-acre park was given to the government of Barbados by Barclays Bank to commemorate independence in 1966. Walk up **Chalky Mount** for magnificent views of the east coast, easily reached at the end of the bus line from Bridgetown. If you ask locally for the exact path you are likely to be given several different routes. Some people say that the Mount looks like the figure of a man resting with his hands over his stomach and it is known locally as 'Napoleon'. While up here you can visit the **Chalky Mount Potteries** in the village, where a potter's wheel of a design that is hundreds of years old is used. You can see the potters at work and buy their produce. Walk down through the meadows to Barclays Park for a drink when you return. Staff in the café will know times of buses to either Bathsheba or Speightstown. The East Coast Road continues a little further north to Long Pond, then skirts Walker's Savannah to Belleplaine, where the railway ended.

★ Bathsheba
East Coast Road, St Joseph. *Map 4, A1, p220*

A sandy beach stretches for miles along the sweeping curve of the coastline from Cattlewash to St Martin's Bay and there are many spots where you can sit and sunbathe, admire the view and do a bit of beachcombing for whatever may have come over from Africa. The tiny hamlet of Bathsheba has a double bay with wave-eroded rocks and boulders at each end and in the middle. The beach is sandy but at the water's edge it turns to flat rocks, which act as platforms, interspersed with rock pools, where you can cool off at low tide.

! Hackleton's Cliff, which runs parallel with the coast inland from Bathsheba, was allegedly named after a man called Hackleton who committed suicide by riding his horse over the cliff.

▶ East coast railway line

A railway was built in 1883 (but closed in 1937) between Bridgetown and Bathsheba. Originally conceived as going to Speightstown, it actually went up the east coast to a terminus at Belleplaine, St Andrew. The cutting at My Lady's Hole, near Conset Bay in St John, is spectacular, with a gradient of 1:31, which is supposed to have been the steepest in the world except for rack and pinion and other special types of line. The railway here suffered from landslides, wave erosion, mismanagment and underfunding so that the 37-mile track was, in places, in very bad condition. The crew would sprinkle sand on the track, while the first class passengers remained seated, the second class walked and the third class pushed. Nowadays, there is good walking along the old railway track. The section from Bathsheba through Bath to Consett Bay is mostly in good condition, although you have to scramble on some bits. It takes about 1½ hours from Bathsheba to Bath, where most people stop to cool off in the sea. South of Consett, there used to be a railway station and sugar factory at Three Houses. The area has now been landscaped and made into a new picnic area, called Three Houses Park.

Windswept and with pounding surf, swimmers confine themselves to these pools which are best in the shelter of the enormous boulders (watch out for sea urchins), but Bathsheba is the place for surfing and the bay seems to be almost white as the surf trails out behind the Atlantic rollers. The popular surf spots are **Soup Bowl** and **Parlour**, where waves break consistently year round but are best between September and November. Surfing championships are often held here. Low key accommodation is available in Bathsheba, the only place on the east coast where you can find anywhere to stay, and there are a few places to eat.

Andromeda Gardens

Above the bay at Hillcrest, Bathsheba, St Joseph, **T** 4339261.
Daily 0900-1700. US$6, children US$3. Map 4, A1, p220

Perched up on the hillside with a fabulous view of the ocean are the Andromeda Gardens, one of Barbados' foremost gardens. They are within walking distance of the beach but it's uphill all the way and hot work. Now owned by the Barbados National Trust, the gardens contain plants from all over Barbados as well as species from other parts of the world, particularly Asia. They were collected by the late Iris Bannochie, who started laying out the garden trails in 1954 alongside a stream, now a prominent water feature. In 1988 she willed the gardens to the National Trust so that they would be open to the public in perpetuity, but they are also affiliated to the University of the West Indies for research and education. There are many varieties of orchid, heliconia, hibiscus and flowering trees and its blooms are regular winners at the Chelsea Flower Show in London. You have a choice of two walks through immaculate gardens, sprawling over the hillside between limestone boulders. It is always full of interest and colour, with good explanatory leaflets for each walk, telling you of the uses of each plant as well as where to stop and rest. The Hibiscus Café has good juices and closes at 1645 in time for staff to catch the 1700 bus back to Bridgetown.

● *For lovers of gardens, two others within reach of Bathsheba are the Flower Forest, see p91 and Orchid World, see p91.*

Bath

St John. *Access is off East Coast Road, just east of Satellite Earth Station. Map 4, B4, p220*

There are a few beach villas at one end, but otherwise this is an empty, unspoilt beach with a long sweep of casuarina trees for shade. The sand is good but at high tide the sea covers it

Life is sweet
It certainly was for the sugar plantation bosses who lived in the lap of luxury in their palatial houses, such as Sunbury, seen here.

completely and you have to retreat into the trees. Low tide is wonderful with rock pools to wallow in for a lovely lazy day. Swimming is reasonably safe here because of an offshore reef, but you have to be careful of the rocks. There's a lifeguard tower for added security. Popular with Bajans at weekends, when families pitch camp around the shaded picnic tables, it is deserted during the week and highly recommended for escaping the crowds. The beach bar usually offers a dish of the day for lunch, often fish fry, or you can get a flying fish sandwich for B$6, chips for B$5, chicken wings or fish cakes for B$0.50 each to fill a nagging hole. Not only is there a children's playground, there is also a large grass area where kids and grown-ups practise football and cricket.

St John's Church
Pothouse, St John. *Map 4, B3, p220*

Perched high up on an 800-ft cliff with views over the Scotland District and the entire rugged east coast, St John's was first built in 1660. However, it was a victim of the great hurricane of 1835 and had to be rebuilt. There is an interesting pulpit made from six different kinds of wood. You will also find the grave of Fernando Paleologus "descendant of ye imperial line of ye last Christian emperors of Greece". The full story is in Leigh Fermor's *The Traveller's Tree*. There are some fine Royal palms in the churchyard, also known as Cabbage palms (roystonea oleracea).

● *The churchyard is interesting to stroll around but pick your moment as it's on the itinerary for island tours and you may be jostling for space with the occupants of the latest cruise ship in port.*

Codrington College
Highway 4b, Parish of St John. *US$2.50. Take the Sargeant St bus as far as Codrington College, then walk 7 miles back along the Atlantic Coast to Bathsheba. Map 4, C4, p220*

This is one of the most famous landmarks on the island and can be seen from Highway 4b down an avenue of Cabbage (Royal) palm trees. It is steeped in history as the first Codrington landed in Barbados in 1628. His son acted as Governor for three years but was dismissed for liberal views. Instead he stood for parliament and was elected speaker for nine years. He was involved in several wars against the French and became probably the wealthiest man in the West Indies. The third Codrington succeeded his father as Governor-General of the Leeward islands, attempted to stamp out the considerable corruption of the time and distinguished himself in various military campaigns (especially in taking St Kitts). He died in 1710, a bachelor aged 42, and left his Barbadian properties to the Society for the

> ## Open gardens

In addition to the spectacular gardens open regularly to the public, Barbados possesses numerous private gardens, lovingly tended by their owners, which are only occasionally open to public scrutiny. Look out for the Barbados Horticultural Society's (BHS) open gardens programme, open 1400-1800 on Sundays in January and February, US$5 including a drink, which are advertised in tourist magazines. There are gardens running down to the sea, gardens up in the hills, gardens which have been created by landscape designers and gardens which have just grown over the years like Topsy.

Barbados has a fine reputation for horticulture and members of the BHS, which has been in existence since 1928, are very keen on their flowers. Barbados regularly exhibits at the Chelsea Flower Show in London in May and usually wins gold medals – a major achievement given the headache of transporting blooms all the way from the Caribbean to the Northern Hemisphere in pristine condition. The BHS holds its own flower show every year in January or February at its headquarters at **Balls Plantation**, Christ Church, T 4285889, where it has 12 acres of landscaped gardens.

Propagation of the Gospel in Foreign Parts. It was not until 1830 that Codrington College, where candidates could study for the Anglican priesthood, was established. From 1875 to 1955 it was associated with Durham University, England. Apart from its beautiful grounds with a huge lily pond and impressive façade, there is a chapel containing a plaque to Sir Christopher Codrington and a library. You can follow the track which drops down 360 ft to the sea at the beautiful Conset Bay.

● *Note that the lily pond flowers close up in the middle of the day.*

East Point Lighthouse
Ragged Point. *Map 4, D7, p220*

The automatic East Point lighthouse stands among the ruined houses of the former lighthouse keepers. There are good views north towards Consett Point, the small Culpepper island, and the south coast. Note the erosion to the 80-ft cliffs caused by the Atlantic sweeping into the coves. An atmospheric station close to the shoreline measures air quality as this is the first landfall after blowing across the Atlantic from the coast of Africa.

Inland

A short way inland from the wild Atlantic coast, but also within easy reach of the west coast, are several stunning gardens and natural attractions such as ancient forests and caves.

◉ Sights

Turners Hall Woods
Parish of St Andrew. *Map 2, I6, p217*

West of Barclays Park and Chalky Mount and reached from St Simon's Church, Turners Hall Woods provide a good vantage point. It is thought that the wood has changed little since the days before the English arrived, although it is less specialized than a true tropical forest, with only 13 species of lianas and three species of epiphyte. The 50-acre patch of tropical mesophytic forest has never been clear-felled (although individual trees were often taken out) and it managed to survive the massive clearance for sugar cane which took place in the 17th century. You can walk over the steep paths here and see many species, ranging from the sandbox tree to the 100-ft locust trees supported by massive buttresses.

This is the only place where you can see Jack-in-the-box trees on Barbados and the forest is a sanctuary for them. The island's first natural gas field was here and the main path through the wood is the remains of the old road.

Flower Forest

Richmond Plantation, St Joseph, **T** 4338152, ffl@sunbeach.net. *Daily 0900-1700. US$7, children 5-16 half price. Combined ticket with Orchid World US$11.50. Turn off Highway 2 on the Melvin Hill road just after the agricultural station and follow the signs. Map 2, J6, p217*

A 50-acre, landscaped former plantation, 850 ft (270 m) above sea level, opened in 1983 with beautifully laid out gardens. The original wooden plantation house, which used to house the snack bar, unfortunately burned down in 1990, so the current administration building was built to replace it. Named paths wend their way around the hillside; they are well-maintained and even suitable for wheelchairs, although there are a few which go off the main tracks and can only be negotiated on foot. The garden contains species not only from Barbados but also from over the world, beautifully arranged with plenty of colour year round. You can find heliconias, ginger lilies, orchids, anthurium, ixoras and bougainvillea as well as productive plants such as bananas, cocoa, coffee and breadfruit. The outstanding feature of this garden, however, is the forest. Enormous trees loom above you, with Royal and other palms giving shade to the paths, while in between you can find bearded fig trees and huge baobab and mango trees. Here and there they open onto large grassy areas affording excellent views over the valley to the east coast. **Liv's Lookout** in particular has a fantastic view right up the northeast seaboard. To the west you can see **Mount Hillaby**, at 1,116 ft (340 m) the island's highest point. The gardeners pride themselves on using only natural fertilizers and no herbicides, except on the orchids, where they use environmentally friendly products. There's also a cafeteria and toilets, and a good information sheet.

Springvale Eco-Heritage Museum

Highway 2, St Andrew, **T** 4387011, newden@sunbeach.net.
1000-1600 Mon-Sat, Sun by appointment. US$5. Map 2, J6, p217

Springvale is an 80-ha former sugar plantation converted into a small folk museum of Barbados with a presentation of historical rural Barbadian life. There's a café serving local juices and food depending on what is in season. It's close to the Flower Forest, so worth a detour if you're in the area. It is very low key and informal. The owner, Newlands Greenidge, can trace his ancestry back to 1631 and a ship which came from Greenwich. He will explain the day-to-day items in the museum, showing how people used to live in colonial times, and will take you along a path outside pointing out the various plants and their uses.

Villa Nova

Map 4, C1, p220 See also Sleeping p108

From Bathsheba you can head inland, driving up Horse Hill to Cotton Tower signal station. Then head south to Wilson Hill where you find Mount Tabor Church and Villa Nova, a plantation Great House dating from 1834. It was once owned by the former British Prime Minister, Sir Anthony Eden, and until 1994 was part of the National Trust's heritage trail. The Queen and Prince Philip visited in 1966 during independence celebrations and planted two portlandias, which have very fragrant blooms. Now a five-star, 28-room country resort hotel, it is the ultimate in luxury country living and perfect for a restful break away from the sea, for a meal or to stay, with lush shady gardens, impeccable decor and an elegant restaurant. Very popular for a long, lazy lunch or

afternoon tea.

Driftwood sculpture
Barbados's beaches range from family-friendly resorts in the south to wild and deserted strands on the Atlantic coast.

Listings

Museums and galleries

- **Barbados Arts Council** Exhibits Barbadian art, see p151.
- **Barbados Museum** The national museum with all facets of Barbadian history, see p54.
- **Beyond Aesthetics Gallery** Art and floral creations by two local artists, see p151.
- **Folkestone Park and Marine Reserve** Small aquatic museum, see p67.
- **Freedom Fine Art Gallery** Original art and prints by local and regional artists, see p151.
- **Gallery of Caribbean Art** Paintings from Barbados and the wider Caribbean, see p151.
- **The Gallery St James** Caribbean and international art and antiquarian maps, see p151.
- **Gang of 4 Art Studio** Art and sculpture by a group of resident artists, see p151.
- **Mallalieu Motor Collection** Vintage car collection, see p55.
- **Mango's Fine Art Gallery** Paintings and prints by Michael Adams, see p152.
- **On the Wall** Regional art exhibited in a restaurant, see p152.
- **Sir Frank Hutson Sugar Machinery Museum** Old machinery and exhibition on sugar making, see p68
- **Springvale Eco-Heritage Museum** Folk museum of rural life, see p92.
- **Sunbury Plantation House** Antique furniture and household artefacts in historical house, see p37.
- **Verandah Art Gallery** Haitian, Cuban and other contemporary Caribbean paintings, see p152.
- **Zemicon Gallery** Local contemporary artists, see p152.

Sleeping

Tourism is the major industry on Barbados and there is a wide selection of hotels, guesthouses, apartments and villas, providing some 8,200 registered and unregistered guest rooms; the aim is to have 10,000 rooms by 2007. Barbados is not for the impecunious, it is an upmarket destination. Visitors come here for a treat and expect – and receive – excellent service and value for money. Unusually for the Caribbean, most of the hotels are independently run. The only big name chain hotel is a newly built *Hilton* on Needham's Point, www.hilton caribbean.com/barbados. Generally, the top hotels in the super luxury category, costing well over US$300 a night, are on the west coast. Places such as *Sandy Lane* are among the world's top resorts, while inland, *Villa Nova* is popular with royalty and rock stars. Cheap and cheerful places can be found on the south coast, but many of these are concrete block, characterless hotels in varying shades of garish colours, usually booked as package holidays. The best 'getaways' are on the rugged, breezy east coast at Bathsheba, where air conditioning is rarely needed and there's little in the way of nocturnal entertainment.

$
Price

Sleeping codes

LL	US$201 and above	**L**	US$151-200
AL	US$101-150	**A**	US$81-100
B	US$61-80	**C**	US$41-60
D	US$31-40	**E**	US$21-30

Price of a double room based on two people sharing. 10% service and 7.5% VAT is levied on hotel services.

Self-catering is popular on Barbados, partly because restaurants are not cheap, and if there is a group of you, you can find good value places to stay. Despite the reputation of the west coast as expensive – it is nicknamed the 'Platinum Coast' – you can find an apartment to rent for as little as US$25 a night per person if you are not too demanding and don't mind walking a few minutes to the beach.

To get a really Bajan feel, look out for renovated chattel houses for rent, see p101. These are becoming more popular and are charming places to stay for a couple or small group. A two-bedroom chattel house rents for around US$70-100 a night, depending on the season, length of stay and proximity to the sea. The decor may not have that 'interior designer' look, but will be of a good standard with all the amenities and equipment you need. Guesthouses are another budget option, some of which are like small hotels but others are more in the line of bed and breakfast in a family house. If meals are available, you can rely on being able to sample local ingredients and recipes.

All-inclusives are to be avoided as the food quickly becomes boring and you will miss out on the fun of selecting from the huge choice of places to eat.

If money's no object, then villa rental is an option. You can have a villa on the beach complete with cook. **Alleyne, Aguillar and Altman**, Derricks, St James, **T** 4320840, www.aaaltman.com, are the most upmarket agents and property managers. **Bajan**

Services, T 4222618, www.bajanservices.com, real estate
agents, property managers and villa rentals, have a range of
luxury properties, most of them beachfront and fully staffed.
Also at the posh end, **Elegant Villas of Barbados**, www.elegant
villasbarbados.com, has 400 short-term properties at US$300-400
a night range for beach cottage and up to US$10,000 a night for
an eight-bedroom villa. **Rival Enterprises Ltd**, Flamboyant Av,
Sunset Crest, St James, T 4326457, rival@caribsurf.com, have
one-bedroom apartments to three-bedroom villas in gardens,
LL-B in season, cheaper in summer, which are well located near
restaurants, shops and the beach.

The **Barbados Tourist Authority**, www.barbados.org, has
a range of brochures, including one on hotels, guesthouses and
apartments and a supplementary brochure on lodging with families
and family apartments around the island. Other websites for small,
low-priced hotels include www.intimatehotelsbarbados.com and
www.shoestringbarbados.com.

South coast

Hotels

LL-L Coral Sands, Worthing Beach, T 4356617,
www.coralsandsresort.com. *Map 3, J5, p219* An attractive
hotel with 31 large oceanfront studios, all with fully-equipped
kitchens, large balconies and good bathrooms, clean, fresh
and elegant but comfortable. Five-minute walk to The Gap
for nightlife, two-minute walk to a good supermarket. No
entertainment at this quiet hotel but the *Carib Beach Bar* is only
100 m away. The area is popular at weekends and the beach can
get dirty. The hotel has a small pool overlooking the broad sandy
beach; no beach chairs.

LL-L The Savannah, Hastings, between Garrison Savannah and beach, **T** 4359473, savannah@gemsbarbados.com. *Map 6, E7, p224* 100 rooms, 21 in a recently renovated historic building which was once the canteen for the Garrison. Each room is different and has antique furniture. Other rooms in new blocks are similar design, very smart with dark wooden furniture and high quality facilities. Recommended for business visitors, there are computer sockets in the rooms, while suites have printers and fax machines, or you can use the business centre. Earth-friendly bathroom goodies, gym, pool, on a rather rocky coastline but its only a short walk to a lovely beach with casuarina trees near the *Hilton* and turtles come here to nest.

LL-AL The Crane, The Crane, St Philip, **T** 4236220, www.the crane.com. *Map 4, H6, p221* Fairly near the airport, but definitely a taxi ride away. Built in 1887 as Barbados' first resort hotel with a spectacular cliff top setting, it is one of the most dramatic in the Caribbean. The Crane has an outstanding beach, good pool, tennis, luxury prices and is usually fairly quiet. Only 18 rooms with antique furnishings and hardwood floors, but an extra 250 timeshare units alongside have changed the character of the hotel.

LL-AL Southern Palms, Christ Church, **T** 4287171, www.southernpalms.net. *Map 3, J6, p219* Short walk to all the restaurants and nightlife of The Gap. Comfortable and unpretentious beach hotel with rooms and spacious suites with kitchenettes. Popular with couples or families, mainly British guests, lovely stretch of beach.

LL-B Silver Sands Resort, Christ Church, **T** 4286001, www.silversandsbarbados.com. *Map 4, L1, p221* 20-minute drive from airport, on the sea at South Point. A dedicated windsurfing resort with a Club Mistral centre open November to June, this is where the serious windsurfers come. 130 rooms and suites, spacious and well-equipped, good service, food dull, good beach but take care swimming, waves are strong, children and weak swimmers should use the pools.

L-AL Island Inn, Aquatic Gap, **T** 4366393, quaint@caribsurf.com. *Map 6, B4, p224* Close to beach, *Brown Sugar* restaurant and the *Hilton*. Good food and service, small and comfortable, very friendly. Built in 1804 as one of the Garrison buildings, now converted with 26 rooms around central courtyard. *Barracks* restaurant and pool. Free glass bottomed boat tour.

AL-C Rostrevor Apartment Hotel, St Lawrence Gap, **T** 4289298, www.barbados.org/hotels/rostrevor. *Map 3, J6, p219* Rooms and apartments, many newly refurbished to a good standard. Family run, friendly staff, not the prettiest hotel but comfortable and in a good location on the beach. Accommodation for wheelchair users in new block, pool, golf packages.

C-E Just Home, Aquatic Gap, **T** 4273265, justhome1@msn.com. *Map 6, C3, p224* Six different a/c rooms from a single sharing a bathroom and kitchenette to a double with private bathroom or a one-bedroom apartment. Conveniently close to Bridgetown if you want to be in that area, next to the *Grand Barbados Hotel* and *Brown Sugar* restaurant, clean and comfortable, run by Caroline Phillips.

Apartments

L-C Chateau Blanc Apartments on Sea, First Av, Worthing, **T** 4357518, www.barbados.org. *Map 3, J6, p219* Right on the beach, apartments range from seafront one to two bedrooms to seaview studios or rooms with kitchenettes. Good value, well-equipped, friendly management.

> ### Chattel houses

Dating from the days of slavery, chattel houses are a distinctive part of Barbados' architectural and social heritage. These wooden houses all conformed to a basic, symmetrical plan, with a central door and a window either side, built on a foundation of loosely packed stones which allowed the air to circulate under and through the house. The steeply-pitched roof would have originally been thatched but later they were all galvanized. Each chattel house was customized by its owners, who added pretty shutters, porches, jalousie windows, verandas and decorative detail such as gingerbread fretwork. The key feature of all chattel houses was that they could all be dismantled and moved easily, so that if a worker moved from one plantation to another he could pack up and move with 'all his goods and chattels'.

Sleeping

AL-A Kabakalli Apartments, Landsdown, Silver Sands, **T** 4282381, kabakalli@funbarbados.com. *Map 4, L2, p221* Named after a tropical hardwood much in evidence in the construction of the building, owned and designed by Patrick Watelet. Three- bedroom apartment upstairs with balcony, louvred windows, shutters, plenty of breeze, very economical for six sharing. Also four one-bedroom apartments with patio and sea view. All with wicker furniture. Great for windsurfers, 200 m from Silver Sands.

AL-B The Nook Apartments, Dayrells Rd in Rockley, **T** 4276502, www.thenookbarbados.com. *Map 3, I5, p219* Apartments and studios, small rooms renovated in 2005, with pool, maid service, TV, phone, clean, secure, convenient for shops and restaurants, two minutes from Accra/Rockley beach.

AL-C Venice Gardens & Bonanza Apartments, 4th Av, Dover, **T** 4289097, bonanza@sunbeach.net. *Map 3, J6, p219* Three buildings: Venice Gardens has eight studios and a two-bedroom apartment, Bonanza has two-bedroom apartments, and Fred La Rose has one-bedroom apartments, tiled floors, simple Bajan furniture. Run by Mrs Lecent Gittens, helpful, quite convenient, *Bean & Bagel* restaurant on the property, short walk to beach.

A-B Southern Heights, 8 Amity Lodge, Worthing, **T** 4358354, www.southernheightsbarbados.com. *Map 3, I5, p219* 12 one-bedroom apartments, a/c, ceiling fan, TV, futon in living/dining room, patio, daily maid service, night watchman, family owned and operated. Not on the beach but convenient for public transport. Sandy Beach is 20 minutes' walk.

B Melrose Beach Apartments, Worthing, **T** 4357985, www.melrosebeach-apts.com. *Map 3, J5, p219* Good location, within walking distance of Sandy Beach and St Lawrence Gap, but on main road, parking, 14 one-bedroom a/c units in pink concrete block, kitchenette, living room, tiled floors, kingsize or twin beds, simple and functional, good value.

B-C Roman Beach Apartments, Enterprise, near Oistins, **T** 4287635, www.romanbeach.com. *Map 3, J8, p219* Friendly, simple, comfortable studios with kitchenette, pretty garden with lots of flowering plants, across the road from beautiful Miami beach, quiet area but close to Oistins for shops and fish fry.

D-E Beach House Cleverdale, Fourth Av, Worthing, **T** 4281035, www.barbados-rentals.com. *Map 3, J5, p219* Looks like a large chattel house from the outside, built in traditional style with wood and stone in a large tropical garden, only 15 m from Sandy Beach.

You can rent rooms or the whole house. There are five double rooms all with high ceilings and wooden floors, the four bigger ones have washbasins, two bathrooms, mosquito screens, large living/dining room with TV, CD, stereo, use of kitchen at the back of the house, small garden, veranda and barbecue for guests to share. Clean and good value, internet access arranged. Run by Germans, Brigette Taylor, **T** 4283172, and Heidrun Rice, karibik@sunbeach.net, who have other properties near the beach where you can rent a room (**E**) or the whole house, simple but adequate accommodation with shared kitchen and garden. Also more upmarket two-bedroom apartments, with communal pool and laundry room, spacious, comfortable, secure, with maid service. Tours and other services arranged.

West coast

Hotels

LL Cobblers Cove, Speightstown, St Peter, **T** 4222291, www.cobblerscove.com. *Map 2, G1, p216* This small and exclusive English country house, a member of Relais & Chateaux, is run by Hamish Watson. It wins lots of awards and a high proportion of repeat business. The 40 spacious suites are elegant but not ostentatious, they also interconnect and are good for families, though no children under 12 are allowed in peak season (from the beginning of January to the end of March). There's a narrow bit of beach with some rocks immediately in front of the hotel, but guests tend to lounge around the kidney-shaped pool instead or head for the watersports area to the side, where there is more sand. Also an elegant French restaurant at the water's edge where a five-course dinner will set you back US$75.

LL Coral Reef Club, Holetown, St James, **T** 4222372, www.coralreefbarbados.com. *Map 2, K1, p217* Very highly regarded family-run hotel with 88 rooms, suites and cottages set in 12 acres of lovely landscaped gardens, with lawns running down to the sea. Some of the villas were rebuilt in 2002 in plantation house style to suit families or couples. Also a beach, pool, tennis, watersports and entertainment most evenings. There's a Bajan buffet on Mondays in the restaurant and a barbecue with steel band and floor show on Thursdays.

LL The House, Paynes Bay, **T** 4325525, www.thehouse barbados.com. *Map 3, C1, p219* The height of luxury where your personal 'ambassador' brings cold towels and drinks to your sunbed and you get a jet lag revival massage on arrival. 32 suites around a courtyard, beautifully decorated and furnished with mahogany and rattan, minibar, fridge and espresso machine, *Daphne's* restaurant alongside, breakfast, tea and canapés included. Well-regarded for service and atmosphere, which is unpretentious, use of facilities of *Tamarind Cove* next door.

LL Little Good Harbour, north of Speightstown, St Peter, **T** 4393000, www.littlegoodharbourbarbados.com. *Map 2, E1, p216* These small wooden villas in traditional gingerbread style around a pool, across the road from the sea, are nicely laid out and furnished but are a bit cramped. There's a good restaurant beside the sea. This place is ideal if you want to be on the west coast but away from the crowds, and Speightstown is handy for shopping, bars and restaurants. Lots of sights in the north are within easy reach but car hire is recommended.

LL Lone Star Motel, on the beach next to the restaurant of the same name, by the Royal Pavilion, St James, **T** 4190599, www.thelonestar.com. *Map 2, J1, p217* A small hotel with a quirky history. It was originally a garage built in 1940s by Romy Reid, who ran a bus company and called himself the Lone Star of the west coast. It was then a nightclub and then a house, owned by Mrs Robertson, of the jam company, who waterskied offshore until her late 80s. It is now an exclusive and barefoot-luxury place to stay with only four huge rooms, uncluttered with simple mahogany furniture. It is right on the beach and within easy reach of Holetown restaurants if you don't always want to eat at the excellent restaurant on site.

LL Sandy Lane, St James, **T** 4442000, www.sandylane.com. *Map 3, B2, p218 See also p105* First opened in 1961 by Ronald Tree, whose own beach house, Heron Bay, could no longer accommodate all the rich and famous people who wanted to stay there, Sandy Lane is synonymous with luxury and an institution in Barbados. However, there was a change of ownership in 1996 and after a period of reflection and planning, the hotel was closed for several years. It reopened in March 2001, having been rebuilt, rather than refurbished, but instead of the previous understated elegance so loved by its regular guests, it is now rather overblown and pretentious, aiming to be the world's premier luxury resort. Still, all the celebrities come here to be pampered.

LL Tamarind Cove, Paynes Bay, **T** 4321332, www.tamarind covehotel.com. *Map 3, C1, p218* 110 large rooms and suites overlooking pleasant gardens leading on to the beach, where there are comfy sun loungers and watersports. Room only or meal plans available, very good food, also *Daphne's* restaurant next door for a romantic dinner. Very comfortable hotel on three floors, spacious balconies, wheelchair access to ground floor rooms, internet access, water taxi to the sister properties in the Elegant Hotels group.

LL-A Sandridge, just north of Speightstown on Heywoods Beach, St Peter, **T** 4222361, www.sandridgehotel.com. *Map 2, G1, p217* Good-sized rooms or family apartments with cooking facilities and north-facing balconies overlooking the pool. Staff and management are friendly, watersports are free for guests and there are good value barbecue evenings. Excellent for families plus a 15-50% discount for internet bookings depending on the time of year.

L-A Sunswept Beach, right on the beach in the heart of Holetown, St James, **T** 4322715, www.sunsweptbeach.com. *Map 2, L1, p217* This is great value for money considering the location, particularly out of high season. Only 23 comfortable rooms with a/c, fan, TV, kitchenettes, reasonable bathrooms and balcony. There is also a small pool in a tiny garden with direct access to the sea (watch the birds bathing in the dripping shower at the gate to the beach). Friendly staff, relaxed with no frills, very convenient (restaurants, banks, shopping centre, bus stop, all within a stone's throw) and a great place to be during Holetown Carnival.

Apartments

AL-C Calypso Rentals, **T** 01356-626620 (UK), www.calypso-rentals.com. *Map 3, C2, p218* Run by Gay Taaffe, who specializes in simple budget apartments and villas on the west coast. Some are right on the beach, others are a five-minute walk away from the water. *Calypso Cottage* is right by *Blue Monkey Beach Bar*, a bright turquoise two-bedroom chattel house with colour-washed floors and painted furniture tucked away behind *Calypso Villa* on the beach at Paynes Bay. It costs US$560-785 a week. *Calypso Villa* is right on the sand, four bedrooms, three bathrooms and sitting room opening on to the small garden with beach access. The daily maid will get your breakfast and a full time cook is available at extra charge. This rents for US$1,475-2,750,

Goods and chattels
The island's architecture is characterized by these funky old chattel houses which can be rented out for a relatively cheap stay.

depending on occupancy and season, a bargain for beachfront property if fully occupied. *Out of the Blue*, Bairds Road, Lower Carlton, St James is a pretty blue chattel house in neat gardens between Holetown and Speightstown near St Albans Beach. With two bedrooms, bathroom, living room, kitchen, fans, TV and outdoor seating, this is excellent value at US$485-590 a week. These places have real character and are highly individual. Get together a group for best value.

A-B Villa Marie, Fitts Village, St James, **T** 4175799, www.barbados.org/villas/villamarie. *Map 3, D2, p218* Three standard double rooms, two large double rooms, of which one can sleep four, and two big apartments with kitchenette also sleeping four. Well-equipped, with huge showers, a large kitchen and a dining room shared by all. Also has a pleasant garden with loungers and mature trees and BBQ. It's only a five-minute walk from the supermarket, local diner, Italian restaurant and beach. Very quiet, gets many repeat guests and is popular with all ages and nationalities. Run by Peter (German) and friendly guard dog Booboo who is left in charge at night. Convenient for public transport but most people hire a car for excursions.

A-C Angler Apartments, Clarke's Rd 1, Derricks, T/F 4320817, www.barbadosahoy.com/angler. *Map 3, D2, p218* Traditional Bajan-style architecture, with 14 studios and one-bedroom apartments, a/c, TV, all with colourfully painted verandas or patios. Restaurant serves freshly made Caribbean vegetarian and seafood dishes and will prepare special meals on request, reservations required. Home-grown vegetables and herbs. Owners live on the premises and priority is given to service, which is friendly and informal, and family orientated. Less than 100 m from the cove with good snorkelling and swimming. Dive or yoga packages can be arranged, also transfers, car hire and reservations.

East coast

Hotels

LL Villa Nova, St John, **T** 4331523, www.villanovabarbados.com. *Map 4, C1, p220 See also p92* A delightful, tranquil 28-suite country hotel with many historical associations, perfect for a few days away from the coast if you can afford it and enjoy peace and quiet. Pleasant pool and gardens with tall, mature trees. Fine dining using local, organic produce. State of the art rain-forest spa opened in 2005 with eight treatment villas and lots of exercise options.

LL-A Edgewater Inn, Bathsheba, **T** 4339900, www.newedge water.com. *Map 4, A1, p220* Large hotel over-looking sea from the top of the cliffs, with 20 a/c rooms and a pool. The style is outdated, with a dark reception area but new management is undertaking a major renovation and upgrading project, adding balconies to the rooms and making it much more attractive. A couple of rooms are particularly sought after for their size and view. Pleasant lunch stop with tables on patio overlooking the ocean. Buffet meals offered some days for tour parties and others.

AL-B Sea-U, Bathsheba, **T** 4339450, www.seaubarbados.com. *Map 4, A1, p220* This is the nicest place to stay on this side of the island, colonial-style wooden house on top of cliffs, seven spacious guesthouse rooms with kitchenettes opening onto a veranda with glorious sea views over the east coast through coconut palms and casuarinas. Two of the rooms are in a separate a/c guest cottage and interconnect to make a two-bedroom cottage (**L**). Run by Uschi (German), family style evening meals served two to three times a week or when four or more people want to eat in, US$23, breakfast US$7, honour bar, lots of hammocks for lounging on the veranda or in the garden, quiet, peaceful, popular with active types who go to bed early.

AL-B Atlantis, Bathsheba, **T** 4339445, www.atlantisbarbados.com. *Map 4, A1, p220* Spectacular setting, opened 1884 alongside railway, now old and tired, feeling effects of Atlantic weather, but worth a visit even if you don't stay in the few rooms available. New owners have given the rooms a face lift, but they remain simple, with basic bathrooms. Traditionally a good place for lunch especially on Sunday (1300) and Wednesday when an excellent buffet meal containing several Bajan dishes is served. Almost an institution and extremely popular with Bajans, so book ahead. Enid Maxwell, who ran it from 1945-2001, has now relinquished the reins.

Sleeping

AL-B Round House Inn, Bathsheba, **T** 4339678,
www.roundhousebarbados.com. *Map 4, A1, p220* The stone
building dates from 1832 and overlooks the sea from the hillside.
In the round part of the house there are four individually furnished
guestrooms. One of them is considerably nicer than the others
with a roof terrace, sky lights, separate shower and toilet but, all
are bright and light. The others are a bit cramped and although
pleasant enough are a bit overpriced. The restaurant is good and
this is the best place to eat in the evenings. Run by Robert and
Gail Manley.

Eating and drinking

There are a number of excellent restaurants on Barbados, with several of gourmet standard. Some of these are in the luxury hotels such as Sandy Lane or Villa Nova, but you don't have to go to a hotel for cordon bleu cuisine. Eating out is not cheap, and restaurants will charge around US$12-40 for a main course, but standards are high and the settings often special, maybe even a table on the beach. The majority of places to eat are clustered around Holetown on the west coast and St Lawrence Gap on the south coast, where there is a wide variety, allowing you to indulge in Italian, Mexican, Indian, French, Japanese or whatever takes your fancy. In Bridgetown there are several cheap canteens for office workers where you can get a filling lunch for US$6, and around the island there are beach bars for lunch, but what is lacking are Bajan restaurants serving cheap, local food in the evenings. A few rumshops sell fried chicken and there are some fast food places but nothing else at the budget end of the scale after dark.

$ **Eating codes**

Price

$$$	US$20 and over
$$	US$10-20
$	US$10 and under

Prices refer to the cost of a main course. VAT is 15%. Service is usually 10%.

Fresh fish is excellent and sold at the markets in Oistins, Bridgetown and elsewhere in the late afternoon and evening, when the fishermen come in with their catch. The main fish season is December to May, when there is less risk of stormy weather at sea. **Flying fish** are the national emblem and a speciality with two or three fillets to a plate, eaten with chips, in a sandwich or with an elegant sauce. Dolphin fish – also called dorado or Mahi Mahi on restaurant menus – and kingfish are larger steak-fish. Snapper is also recommended and sea eggs (the roe of the white sea urchin) are delicious but not often available as they are increasingly rare and in need of protection.

Other tasty specialties include **cou-cou**, a filling starchy dish made from breadfruit or corn meal, and **jug-jug**, a Christmas speciality made from guinea corn and supposedly descended from the haggis of the poor white settlers. **Pudding and souse** is a huge dish of pickled breadfruit, black pudding and pork.

Oistins on a Friday night is a major event for both Bajans and tourists. Lots of small shops sell fish meals and other food, dub music one end and at the other a small club where they play oldies for ballroom dancing. It continues on Saturday and Sunday, though a bit quieter, and some food places also stay open through the week.

Ripe for the picking

There is a riot of tropical fruit and vegetables, with the exotic and unidentifiable as well as more familiar items found in supermarkets in Europe and North America but with ten times the flavour. The best bananas in the world are grown in the Caribbean on small farms using the minimum of chemicals, if not organic. They are cheap and incredibly sweet and unlike anything you can buy at home. You will come across in juices or in ice cream many of the wonderful tropical fruits. Don't miss the rich flavours of the soursop, the guava or the sapodilla. Mangoes in season drip off the trees and those that don't end up on your breakfast plate can be found squashed in abundance all over the roads. Caribbean oranges are often green when ripe, as there is no cold season to bring out the orange colour, and are meant for juicing not peeling, while portugals are like tangerines and easy to peel. Avocados are also plentiful, as is the the breadfruit, a common staple rich in carbohydrates and vitamins A, B and C, was brought from the South Seas in 1793 by Captain Bligh, perhaps more famous for the mutiny on the Bounty.

South coast

\$\$\$ Champers, Hastings, **T** 4356644, champers@caribsurf.com. *Mon-Sat 1130-late.   Map 3, J4, p219* Waterfront bar and bistro downstairs, dining room upstairs on balcony. The bar is popular and lively and a pleasant place to have a drink listening to the waves breaking below. Champagne, by the way, costs from US\$60 a bottle.

$$$ David's Place, St Lawrence Main Rd, Worthing, **T** 4359755, www.davidsplacebarbados.com. *Tue-Sun 1800-2200 Map 3, J6, p219* On the waterfront looking across the bay to the lights of *Pisces* at night. Barbadian cuisine, one of the better places to eat. Dress smartly.

$$$ Josef's, St Lawrence Gap, **T** 4207638, josefsrestaurant@ hotmail.com. *Dinner only 1830-2200. Map 3, J6, p219* Small, delightful and well used by Barbadians, so you need to book well ahead. Arrive early and have pre-dinner drinks on the lawn with the sea lapping the wall a few feet below you. Candlelit elegance combined with delicious food. Caribbean and Asian flavours, tapas lounge on upstairs terrace.

$$$ Pisces, St Lawrence Gap, **T** 4356564, piscesrestaurant@ caribsurf.com. *From 1830. Map 3, J6, p219* Perfect candlelit waterfront setting with waves lapping beneath you, good fish dishes – flying fish US$19, lobster US$38 – and an excellent vegetarian platter. Very popular and the staff are rushed off their feet, so the service suffers.

$$$ Zafran, El Sueño mansion, Worthing Main Rd, Worthing, Christ Church, **T** 4358995, www.barbados.org/rest/zafran. *Lunch Tue-Sun, dinner Mon-Sat. Map 3, J5, p219* Indian, Persian and Thai food, prepared by Indian chefs. Come here for your tandoori, biryani, balti or vegetarian curry. A three-course lunch is US$19. You can have wine and tapas upstairs in the bell tower or the late night lounge bar, or take afternoon tea on the croquet lawn.

$$$-$$ Bellini's Trattoria, Little Bay Hotel, St Lawrence Gap, **T** 4357246. *1800-2230. Map 3, J6, p219* Lovely waterfront setting on the bay opposite Pisces with its pretty lights reflecting on the water. Italian menu, fresh pasta, but not just spaghetti and pizza, food average, come here for the view of the bay and boats.

A taste of the Caribbean

There are hundreds of different rums in the Caribbean, each island producing the best, of course. Barbados is one of the main producers and you can find some excellent brands. Generally, the younger, light rums are used in cocktails and aged, dark rums are drunk on the rocks or treated as you might like a single malt whisky. Barbados rum is probably the best in the English-speaking Caribbean, unless of course you come from Jamaica, or Guyana. It is worth paying a bit extra for a good brand such as *VSOP* or *Old Gold*, or for the slightly sweeter Sugar Cane Brandy, unless you are going to drink it with Coca Cola, in which case anything will do. A rum and cream liqueur, *Crisma*, is popular in cocktails or on the rocks. Mount Gay produce a vanilla and a mango flavoured rum. *Falernum* is sweet, sometimes slightly alcoholic, with a hint of vanilla and great in a rum cocktail instead of sugar syrup. Corn and oil is rum and falernum. *Mauby* is bitter, made from tree bark and non-alcoholic. It is watered down like a fruit squash and can be refreshing with lots of ice. *Sorrel* is a bright red Christmas drink made with hibiscus sepals and spices; it is very good with white rum.

$$ 39 Steps, Chattel Plaza, Hastings, on the coast road near the Garrison, **T** 4270715, joe.s@caribsurf.com. *1200-2400 Mon-Fri, 1800-2400 Sat, closed Sun. Map 6, F7, p224* Well run and lively bistro and wine bar, imaginative blackboard menu and choice of indoors or balcony tables, pasta, steak, fish and pizza. Popular, so book at weekends. Live jazz every other Saturday.

$$ Café Sol, St Lawrence Gap, **T** 4359531, cafesol@ funbarbados.com. *1800-2300, happy hours 1800-1900, 2200-2300. Map 3, J6, p219* Grill and margarita bar with 15 flavours of margaritas to satisfy anyone's preferences. Seating is partly indoors, partly outside and the restaurant is on the street corner so if you sit outside you can keep an eye on what is going on in The Gap. It is always crowded and very popular. The Tex-Mex menu offers the usual tacos and tortillas, with a 10% discount for takeaway.

$$ Carib Beach Bar, 2nd Av, Worthing, **T** 4358540. *Lunch and dinner. Map 3, J5, p219* Inexpensive meals and drinks, barbecue and music twice a week, and excellent rum punches. Happy hour is 1700-1800 Monday to Friday and great fun, even if you're not eating.

Bridgetown and around

$$$ Brown Sugar, Bay St, Aquatic Gap, **T** 4267684. *Daily 1800-2130 and Sun-Fri 1200-1430. Map 6, C3, p224* Filling and hearty Bajan specialities at dinner in an attractive setting with lots of greenery and a waterfall. Also an all-you-can-eat Bajan buffet lunch for around US$20 Sunday to Friday.

$$$ Lobster Alive Bistro & Beach Bar, on beach next to Boatyard on Bay St, Carlisle Bay, **T** 4350305. *1200-2100. Map 5, H11, p223* Mostly lobster flown in from the Grenadines, but also other seafood and delivery. Quite a good place to eat if you are going on to the Boatyard for entertainment later, but not a cheap option.

$$$ Waterfront Café, on the Careenage, **T** 4270093, www.waterfrontcafe.com.bb. *Food served 0900-2200, drinks till 2400, closed Sun. Map 5, E8, p223* Plenty to look at from the balcony overlooking the boats and the bridge and a good social centre in the evenings. Live entertainment most nights. The food is reasonable with an interesting menu and a good Caribbean buffet on Tuesdays for US$22.50 with steel pan.

$ Balcony Upstairs, in Cave Shepherd on Broad St, **T** 4312088. *Lunch Mon-Fri 1100-1500. Map 5, D7, p223* Canteen-style Bajan lunch popular with office workers. Lots of carbohydrate and root vegetables. You'll probably have to ask what some of the dishes are.

$ Christie's Canteen, at Light and Power Company, on Bay St and at Spring Gardens. *Lunch only. Map 6, C4, p224* Open to the public although it is a staff canteen. Serves a huge traditional lunch with plenty of choice and lots of filling food.

$ De Kitchen, Lower Bay St near the boatyard, **T** 4272214. *Lunch Mon- Fri 1100-1500. Map 5, H10, p223* Good, filling, local food, they do a combo plate for US$7. It's cheaper than eating in the tourist spots if you are spending the day on the beach.

$ Mustor's Harbour, McGregor St, **T** 4265175. *Mon-Fri 0900-1600. Map 5, D5, p222* Third generation family business. Snackette downstairs with Bajan fishcakes etc, and restaurant upstairs serving tasty, filling Bajan food. A good place to stop after a mornings shopping or sightseeing trip to town.

$ Pop's Place, on Cheapside Rd, **T** 4305979. *Lunch Mon-Fri 1100-1500. Map 5, C1, p222* Nice setting, very clean, and only US$7 for a good, filling lunch. You probably won't need to eat again that day. Not far from the market and the bus station for the west coast.

$ Port Hole, Fontabelle, near Barbados Tourist Authority, **T** 4269737. *Lunch Mon-Fri 1100-1500. Map 5, D1, p222* Friendly bar serving a good, solid lunch for US$6. It's mainly used by office workers, so not open weekends. Not far from the Pelican Craft Centre if you are shopping for souvenirs and within walking distance of the Kensington Oval for cricket fans.

Best

★ **Cheap eats**

- Oistins fish fry on Fridays, p42
- Fisherman's Pub, p125
- Christie's Canteen, p118
- Mustor's Harbour, p118
- Fried chicken at a Baxters Road rumshop, p132

$ Tim's, 43 Swan St, **T** 2280645. *Lunch Mon-Fri 1100-1500. Map 5, C7, p223* Local food with lots of carbohydrate, but an opportunity to try things you won't be offered on a restaurant menu. It is canteen style, so you choose what you fancy, at US$2-3 per portion, eat in or takeaway. There's seating on the balcony overlooking the shoppers on Swan Street, or indoors with air conditioning. Gets busy at lunchtime with office workers.

West coast

Restaurants

$$$ The Cliff, Derricks, St James, **T** 4321922. *Mon-Sat, Sun in high season, dinner only. Map 3, D1, p218* Expensive but worth the prices for a glimpse of the decor and great at sunset looking over the Caribbean Sea. One of several restaurants recommended as the best food on the island and they do offer an attractive and delightful meal with stunning desserts. Reservations are essential. Sometimes closed for private functions. Chef Paul Owens has a team of 12 chefs striving for excellence.

$$$ Daphne's, Paynes Bay, St James, **T** 4322731. *1200-1500, 1830-2230, cocktail bar open from 1200. Map 3, C2, p218* Chic and contemporary Italian that is currently a favourite place to eat. The emphasis is on simple, fresh ingredients and lots of seafood. Try to get a waterfront table when booking. Sister property to *Daphne's* in Chelsea, London.

$$$ La Mer, Port St Charles Marina, St Peter, **T** 4192000, lamer@ caribsurf.com. *Lunch Tue-Fri, dinner Mon-Sat. Map 2, E1, p217* Waterfront dining overlooking the lagoon and the yachts berthed outside luxury apartments. Dinner is an elaborate affair. Lunch is relatively cheap at US$15. Sunday brunch at 1200 is very popular.

$$$ Lone Star, Mount Standfast, St James, right on the beach just north of Royal Pavilion hotel, **T** 4190599, www.thelonestar.com. *Daily for lunch and dinner, last orders 2230. Map 2, J1, p217* This is one of the best restaurants, as reflected in the prices, but not ruinous if you choose carefully. It distinguished by having the only caviar bar on the island with three types of caviar from Iran. Lunch can cost anything from US$25-2,000, depending on how much caviar you eat. Sushi, oriental and Asian dishes as well as Caribbean, or you can have shepherd's pie or fish and chips with peas. It is a wonderful setting at beach level, with plenty of space. Michael Winner described it as 'The Ivy of the Caribbean', but luckily the waiting list for a table is not as long as at London's premier restaurant.

$$$ Mango's by the Sea, Speightstown, **T** 4220704, www.mangosbythesea.com. *Dinner only, from 1800, kitchen closes at 2145. Map 2, G1, p217* Nice waterfront setting in an old wooden building, which is romantic as the sun goes down. The menu features mostly seafood and very fresh fish, but several vegetarian options are also available which are more unusual than some places. Complimentary shuttle from all points north of Holetown. Run by Canadians, Gail and Pierre Spenard.

$$$ Mannie's Suga Suga, Mullins Bay, just south of Speightstown, St Peter, **T** 4223892. *Daily 0900-2200, no dinner Thu, Sun. Map 2, H1, p217* What was once a beach bar has become very posh, with sun lounger service on the beach and a restaurant overlooking the sand. Meals and snacks served all day. Monday nights there is a cabaret show, US$3 cover charge. Japanese and Thai food.

$$$ Olives, 2nd St, Holetown, St James, **T** 4322112, olives@caribsurf.com. *Mon-Sat 1830-2200. Map 3, B1, p218* Mediterranean/Caribbean cuisine in a bistro atmosphere in an old Barbadian house. You can order pizza or pasta from US$14-22, but the other main courses are more expensive. Pudding lovers must try the bread and butter pudding with toffee brandy sauce. You can eat inside with air conditioning, or outside in the courtyard. Smoking or non-smoking areas. The lounge bar upstairs has snack meals and pizza and is open until late.

$$$ The Terrace, Cobblers Cove Hotel, **T** 4222291, www.cobblerscove.com. *Breakfast, lunch and dinner. Map 2, G1, p216.* Elegant French dining on the terrace by the pool, overlooking the sea. Friday evening seafood and caviar. Mostly local ingredients used. A five-course dinner costs US$75.

$$$ The Tides, Holetown, **T** 4328356, www.tidesbarbados.com. *Mon-Fri lunch, Mon-Sat dinner, reservations required. Map 3, A1, p218* Seafood, meat and vegetarian dishes, served on an oceanfront terrace, a/c lounge for drinks. Very highly thought of, one of the best restaurants on the island. Home to *On The Wall* art gallery.

$$$-$$ Angry Annie's, 1st St, Holetown, St James, **T** 4322119. *Mon-Sat 1800-2200. Map 3, B1, p218* A lively and popular place in the heart of Holetown. Very colourful with brightly painted furniture. The sociable Brummie host, Paul Matthews, will lend you his red reading glasses if you can't see the menu. Excellent garlic shrimp, jump-up ribs a bit sweet but OK, also steak, lobster, rack of lamb, curries and good salad.

$$$-$$ The Fish Pot, at Little Good Harbour Hotel, north of Speightstown, St Peter, **T** 4392604. *Breakfast, lunch and dinner. Map 2, E1, p216* Nice setting in 18th-century Fort Rupert overlooking the water. The imaginative menu features mostly seafood, and you may want to splash out on the lobster salad. Dinner is from US$20 and reservations are advised.

$$$-$$ Ragamuffins, 1st St, Holetown, **T** 4321295, raga@caribsurf.com. *Dinner only. Map 3, B1, p218* In a chattel house with indoor or outdoor seating. Seafood, West Indian curries, steak and vegetarian dishes, with daily specials.

$$ Cocomos, Holetown, St James, **T** 4320134. *1200-2300. Map 3, B1, p218* On the beach. They have a varied and interesting menu, featuring salads, seafood, steak, burgers and pasta. It's all good, solid food. Spacious and airy, quick service, pleasant staff and nice atmosphere. Happy hour 1600-1800.

$$ Jumbo's, 1 Clarke's Gap, Derricks, St James, **T** 4328032. *Closed Mon, Fri lunch only, Sat, Sun dinner only. Map 3, D2, p218* Chattel conversion with added veranda. Good wine list and reasonable prices (lunch buffet US$12.50). Adventurous food with Thai and Japanese influences, as well as Bajan.

$$ The Mews, 2nd St, Holetown, St James, **T** 4321122. *1830-2300, Sun in season only, bar open till late. Map 3, B1, p218* Superb food with a mix of local and French dishes, served in a very pretty old house, with tables on the balcony or on the interior courtyard patio. The bar is popular after dinner, particularly on Fridays when there is live entertainment.

Rum cocktails

Cocktails first became popular after the development of ice-making in the USA in 1870, but boomed in the 1920s partly because of prohibition in the USA and the influx of visitors to Cuba, the Bahamas and other islands, escaping stringent regulations. People have been drowning their rum in cola ever since the Americans brought bottled drinks in to Cuba during the war against Spain at the end of the 19th century, hence the name, **Cuba Libre**. Rum can be used to substitute other spirits in any cocktail recipe. One of the nicest and most refreshing cocktails is a **Daiquirí**, invented in Santiago de Cuba in 1898 by an engineer in the Daiquirí mines. The natural version combines 1½ tablespoons of sugar, the juice of half a lime, some drops of maraschino liqueur, 1½ oz light dry rum and a lot of shaved ice, all mixed in a blender and then served piled high in a wide, chilled champagne glass with a straw. You can also have fruit versions,

with strawberry, banana, peach or pineapple, using fruit or fruit liqueur. Everybody has heard of the old favourite, **Piña Colada**, which can be found on all the islands and is probably the most popular of the fruit-based cocktails, ideal by the side of the pool. Combine and blend coconut liqueur, pineapple juice, light dry rum and shaved ice, then serve with a straw in a glass, a pineapple or a coconut. The standard recipe for a **rum punch** is: 'one of sour, two of sweet, three of strong and four of weak'. If you measure that in fluid ounces, it comes out as 1 oz of lime juice, 2 oz of syrup (equal amounts of sugar and water, boiled for a few minutes), 3 oz of rum and 4 oz of water, fruit juices, ginger ale, or whatever takes your fancy. You could add ice and a dash of Angostura Bitters from Trinidad, use nutmeg syrup from Grenada or Falernum from Barbados instead of sugar syrup, and garnish it with a slice of lime.

$$ Pizzaz, Chattel Village, Holetown, St James, **T** 4320227, deliveries **T** 4274002. *1200-2300. Map 3, B1, p218* Good fast food, pizza, pasta, samosas, subs, fish or chicken and chips. Try the Bajan pizza, which has flying fish and plantain on it and comes in three sizes from US$12.50 to US$20.50.

$$ Sitar, 2nd St, Holetown, St James, **T** 4322248. *Open for lunch and dinner. Map 3, B1, p218* For those who can't do without a tandoori or hot vindaloo, this is the place to come to satisfy those urges. There aren't many places on the island selling Indian food, but Sitar is worth seeking out. Vegetarian lunch buffet is US$15.

$$-$ Asian Palm, 1st St, Holetown, **T** 4327939. *1100-1430, 1700-2200. Map 3, B1, p218* Thai restaurant and bar, takeaway service available. Casual dining upstairs on the balcony or downstairs by the bar. Wide selection of dishes taking in local ingredients such as flying fish and lobster, also vegetarian dishes.

$$-$ Café Indigo, Highway 1, Holetown, opposite the Methodist Church, **T** 4320968. *0830-1700 for breakfast and lunch, dinner Tue, Thu till 2045. Map 3, B1, p218* Upstairs in an old building. Full English breakfast US$10, pub lunch US$8-12.50, soup, pâté, pies and pizza, steak, prawns and fish. Has a well-stocked bar.

$$-$ Surfside, Holetown Beach, St James, **T** 4322105. *Happy hour 1600-1700. Map 3, B1, p218* On the sand, typical beach bar with seats outside or under cover. All-day breakfast, burgers, rotis, soup and main meals. Daily specials. Daiquiris in various flavours, US$5. Basic and cheerful.

$$-$ The Tree House, Earthworks Pottery, Edgehill Heights No 2, St Thomas, **T** 4252890, treehouse@sunbeach.net. *Mon-Fri 0900-1700, Sat 100-1430. Map 3, C4, p218* Time your shopping trip to the pottery so you can have lunch with a wonderful view from the veranda over the coast. Marguerite Moe runs one of the best cafés on the island, offering imaginative salads, sandwiches, panini, focaccia, pita bread, cakes, juices, smoothies, iced or hot teas and coffees, soups in winter, all delicious, beautifully presented on Earthworks' tableware.

$ Fisherman's Pub, Speightstown, **T** 4222703. *Daily 1000-1600, dinner 1800-2130, Sun till 2200, happy hour 1600-1800. Map 2, G1, p216* Good, no frills meal for US$7, right on seafront by the jetty. No table service. Order and pay for your food at the bar, take the ticket and then hand it in at the kitchen. On Wednesday nights dinner is from 1900 with a steel band and floor show from 2000 on the deck over the sea; diners US$17.50, non-diners US$2.50.

$ Patisserie Flindt, 1st St, Holetown, St James, **T** 4322626. patisserieflindt@caribsurf.com. *Mon-Fri 0700-1700, and Thu, Fri 1830-2130, Sat 0700-1400, Sun 0700-1200. Map 3, B1, p218* Also smaller outlet at Quayside Centre, Rockley, **T** 4352600. *Mon-Wed 1000-1800, Thu-Sat 1000-2130.* Two locations but the Holetown is the larger, with seating for breakfast, lunch or tea, or a snack at any time of day. The cakes, desserts and sweets in the patisserie are divine but pricey – a delicious and luxurious treat – and the hand-made chocolates are out of this world. Sandwiches, salads and pasta are on offer at lunchtime and at weekends they do a full English breakfast for US$10. Picnics can be made to order. Ideal for an event such as the Holders Season.

Eating and drinking

East coast

$$ Atlantis, Bathsheba, **T** 4339445, www.atlantisbarbados.com. *1230-1500, 1800-1930. Map 4, A1, p220* Specializing in Bajan food, you can find all the typical dishes here. A three-course lunch is US$17.50 and a three-course dinner US$22.50, with several options, lots of fish and chicken, followed by local desserts including Enid Maxwell's coconut cream pie. To try a wider range of Bajan dishes came for the buffet lunch on Wed, US$22.50, or the more sumptuous buffet on Sun, US$25, at 1300, reservations required.

$$ Naniki, Surinam, St Joseph, **T** 4331300, www.lushlife.bb. *1000-sundown, lunch 1200-1500, tea 1600-1800, full moon dinners by prior arrangement. Take the turning off Highway 3 just south of St Joseph's church, where there are signs to Lush Life Nature Resort (Naniki). Map 2, K8, p217* Difficult to get to but well worth the effort. Bajan-style cooking with local ingredients, much of it organic. The restaurant is perched on a hillside overlooking the Atlantic Coast, with a tremendous view over fields and palm trees. There is an anthurium farm on the property and lodges for accommodation were built in 2005. The restaurant is cool and airy and you can eat on the deck or inside. A special place, run by Tom Hinds.

$$ Round House Inn, Bathsheba. *0800-1000, 1130-1500, 1830-2100, closed Sun night. Map 4, A1, p220* Lovely restored building dating from 1832 and overlooking the sea. This is the best place to eat at night in the area, with interesting food using unusual combinations of ingredients and tasty starters. There's jazz on Wednesday nights, reggae on Saturdays and a guitarist Sunday lunchtimes in season.

Barbados stays as busy after dark as it does during the day, when all those people who spent their day lying on the beach move into the bars and clubs. Beach bars can be lively both day and night, often with live music and dancing. There is quite a selection of places to while away the midnight hours, with a variety of live bands and DJs in the bars, clubs and sports bars all along the west and south coasts, particularly St Lawrence Gap, known as the 'hip strip', where there are around 40 bars, restaurants, pubs and clubs offering entertainment. This isn't Ibiza, where you can party until breakfast. People are going to bed earlier than they used to and no longer catch the first bus home. However, most clubs open around 2200 but do not get lively until almost midnight, and close around 0200-0400. Most charge US$12.50 or more for entry on 'free drinks' night; less when you are paying for the drinks. It's worth phoning in advance to find out what's on offer, as well as find out about any dress codes or admission rules.

Look in the fortnightly magazine, *Friends*, free in most hotels, for information about what's on, or try some of the websites such as www.bajandancehall.com for parties and bashments (parties, raves or gigs). If you haven't had enough of the sea during the day, you can join a party cruise and dance the night away aboard the *Jolly Roger* or the *Harbour Master*, usually a riotous, drunken affair.

For something authentically Bajan it might be worth trying one of the **dances** which are advertised in the *Nation* newspaper on Friday. This involves ballroom dancing to slows and 'back in times'. People hire a dance hall, charge admission (usually US$5), provide a disco, and keep the profits. There are very few foreigners, but the atmosphere is friendly, and the drinks a lot cheaper than in the smarter nightclubs. A more permanent home for this sort of thing is the beautifully named *Lonely Hearts*, upstairs opposite the Treasury Building Close, just off Heroes Square in Bridgetown.

There are also **fêtes**, which attract a younger crowd and Jamaican-style dub music, advertised by poster and sometimes on the radio. Venues include *Penthouse*, close to Parliament buildings in Bridgetown, *Cactus* in Silver Sands, *Liberty* in Black Rock and *De Base* on Bay Street in Bridgetown. Unfortunately, there have been a few fights at 'Dub' fêtes and they are not as relaxed as they used to be.

South coast

Bars

After Dark, St Lawrence Gap, **T** 4356547. *2200-0300. Map 3, J6, p219* Very lively bar with a huge selection of drinks attracting more Bajans than tourists. DJ every night but live music quite often.

Bubba's Bar, Rockley, **T** 4356217. *1000-2200. Map 3, I5, p219* With a 10-ft video screen plus 10 other TVs for watching sports while you drink.

Carib Beach Bar, 2nd Av, Worthing, **T** 4358540. *Happy hour Mon-Fri 1700-1800. Map 3, J5, p219* A fun place to eat and drink all day and into the night. Popular on Sunday nights when local people come to dance to the DJ. Move out onto the sand if you want a quieter time.

Chiller's, north side of main road opposite Sandy Beach, Worthing. *Map 3, J5, p219* A lively pub with music and dancing. No entry charge.

Cool's Castaways Cocktail Bar, St Lawrence Gap, **T** 4270965. *1730 till late. Map 3, J6, p219* Blues and jazz bar, live music, design your own cocktail.

Ship Inn, St Lawrence Gap, **T** 4207447. *Daily 1200- late, happy hour 1600-1800. US$10 some nights. Map 3, J6, p219* Large outdoor area which is often packed, especially at weekends, and where you can hear calypso and reggae, mixed in with other styles. Different live events nearly every night.

Clubs

Club Xtreme, Worthing, Christ Church, **T** 4354455. *2100-0300, Fri till 0400. Map 3, J5, p219* Dress code casual but no hats. Old Dub Tuesdays, ladies' night and special events on Fridays, admission after 2230 US$20, first 100 ladies get free glow sticks. Resident DJs play the latest dance, hip hop, reggae and calypso. ID enforced.

McBride's Irish Pub, St Lawrence Gap, **T** 4207646, mcsoul@ sunbeach.net. *Map 3, J6, p219* DJ or live music every night in the air-conditioned dance club from 2230. This is Irish owned and operated and although most of the food is international there are traditional Irish specialities. Also a games room with pool tables. Look out for their pub quizzes, karaoke, reggae rock, Latin dancing, back in time dancing or DJ evenings.

Reggae Lounge, St Lawrence Gap, **T** 4356462. *2100 till late, happy hour 1000-2200. Map 3, J6, p219* A bit sleazy but can be fun nevertheless. Mondays US$15 (ladies US$12.50 before 2300), drinks free; Thursdays live music, US$12.50 before 2300, US$15 after (ladies US$5 before 2200). Fridays dusk till dawn dance party, US$2.50 before midnight, US$5 afterwards. Most Saturdays there is live entertainment, US$5 (ladies free before 2200). Lots of reggae as the name suggests, with bands such as *2nd Ave*, *Coalishun* and *Sudden Impact*. Events change seasonally but can be checked in the weekly 'what's on' section in *Friends* magazine.

Bridgetown and around

Bars

The Waterfront Café, the Careenage, Bridgetown, **T** 4270093, www.waterfrontcafe.com.bb. *1800-late. Map 5, E8, p223* A bar/restaurant with live entertainment Monday to Saturday, classical guitar, piano music, vocals, big band, jazz or steel pan.

Clubs

Boatyard, Bay St, Bridgetown, **T** 4362622, www.theboatyard.com. *2030-0100. Map 5, H11, p223* The sailor's pub in front of the anchorage at Carlisle Bay, free drinks on Tuesdays, US$17.50 with a live band, sunset beach party on Wednesdays, after work wind down on Fridays with entertainment, US$5, happy hours 1700-1900, 2100-2300, entertainment parties on Saturdays, cover charge varies. Very lively all week, popular with landlubbers too. Plays calypso and reggae as well as international hits.

Harbour Lights, Marine Villa, Bay St, Bridgetown, **T** 4367225, www.harbourlightsbarbados.com. *US$15, US$17.50 Fri. No cover*

▶ Rum place for a drink

The traditional place to drink has always been the rumshop, a one-roomed shack found on every street corner where the men gathered to discuss the events of the day, the results of the cricket match and the latest political gossip.

In a rumshop, rum and other drinks are bought by the bottle. The smallest size is a mini, then a flask, then a full bottle. The shop will supply ice and glasses, you buy a mixer, and serve yourself.

The same system operates in dances, though prices are higher. Nightclubs, of course, serve drinks by the glass like anywhere else. Wine in a rumshop usually means sweet British sherry. And be careful as it is drunk with ice and beer.

Baxters Road, in Bridgetown, used to be the place to go but there are fewer people there now and the Government plans to upgrade it as a tourist attraction. These ramshackle rumshops are open all night (literally), and there's a lot of street life after midnight, although you might get pestered by cocaine addicts. Some of the rumshops sell fried chicken. The *Pink Star* is recommended as it has a large indoor area where you can eat in peace and the place also has clean lavatories.

There are also women in the street selling fish, seasoned and fried in coconut oil over an open fire. This is especially recommended if you are hungry after midnight.

Nelson Street rumshops are really houses of ill repute but have amazing larger-than-life naif paintings on the outside, while the interior upstairs bar decor is a curious mix of gillie pix, fluorescent pointillist and life-size portraits of politicians.

charge Sun or Thu. Map 3, I4, p219 Fun, open-air venue on the beach, with local and disco music. For a younger crowd with lots of tourists and expats. Cover charge includes 'free' drinks on

Wednesday 2100-0200. Friday is DJ music night. Beach party with dinner on Monday and Wednesday 1900-2230, when all ages are welcome. Entertainment includes stiltmen, limbo dancing, Green Monkey, Shaggy Bear and the Fire Eater. Hotel transfers can be arranged.

Harbour Master, The Shallow Draught, Bridgetown, **T** 4300900, www.tallshipcruises.com. *Tue-Thu 1100-1600, 1800-2200. Map 3, G2, p219* A floating fun palace, 100 ft long and 40 ft wide with four decks like a Mississippi paddle steamer. Unlike the other cruises, it pulls up on the beach. During the day it rolls out the Malibu Splash water slide and is a semi-submersible, while at night there is limbo dancing and a floor show as well as live music and a DJ during the dinner cruise.

Jolly Roger, **T** 4300900, www.tallshipcruises.com. *Map 3, G2, p219* Four-hour daytime and evening pirate-themed cruises from the deepwater harbour along the west coast to Holetown. This is where the fun and games take place, with walking the plank, swinging on a rope, and other such piratical pranks. The drinks are plentiful and very definitely unlimited. There is also a meal, music and dancing. It costs US$55 for the dinner cruise. On daytime cruises there is swimming and snorkelling.

West coast

Bars

Coach House, Paynes Bay, St James, **T** 4321163. *1700-0200, happy hour 1700-1900. Map 3, C2, p218* Lively pub with international sporting events shown on satellite TV. Steel pan music is played on Tuesdays and Wednesdays, reggae on Mondays, calypso on Thursdays and Saturdays, and then things take a turn for the worse with karaoke on Sundays. There's also international music most nights.

Daphne's, Paynes Bay, St James, **T** 4322731. *Cocktail bar open from 1200. Map 3, C2, p219* Also a restaurant, see p119, the bar is cosy and comfortable with sofas, armchairs and other seating. Extensive cocktail and wine list, the passion fruit martini is to die for.

Fisherman's Pub, Speightstown, St Peter, **T** 4222703. *From 1000. Map 2, G1, p217* Right on the seafront by the jetty, this place offers a no-frills night out with no table service. Dinner is from 1800-2130, except Sundays 1800-2200 and Wednesday nights when dinner is served from 1900 with a steel band and floor show from 2000 (US$17.50 for diners; US$2.50 non-diners). Happy hour 1600-1800.

The Mews, 2nd St, Holetown, **T** 4321122. *Dinner Mon-Sat 1830-2300, bar open till late. Map 3, B1, p219* Mainly known as a restaurant, see p122, but also a popular bar. Good after-dinner drinking spot. Lively at the weekend; live entertainment on Friday.

Clubs

Casbah, Holetown, St James, **T** 4322258, baku@sjds.net. *2100-0200. Map 3, B1, p218* The best place on the west coast, otherwise known as Baku because it is in the same building as La Terra and Baku restaurants. It is billed as 'European style' and 'Moroccan themed', and is more sophisticated than some of the other places on the south coast, with fewer teenage tourists and popular with those in their 20s and 30s. It is perhaps quieter than some other clubs although you still can't hear yourself think and it can get packed. The setting is glorious, right beside the sea with the waves lapping below. Get a table lit by fairy lights overlooking the water; it's very romantic. Free drinks on Thursdays, Latin beat on Wednesdays, plus excellent live music some nights with local bands.

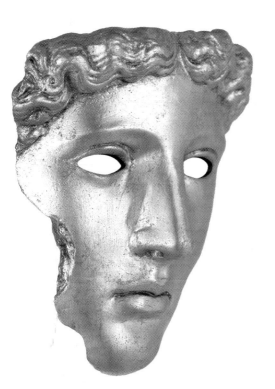

Barbados is not short of entertainment and there is always something going on somewhere, whether of the home-grown or imported variety. The island has produced musicians of excellent quality, both writers and performers of calypso, reggae, soca, gospel and other Caribbean styles, who play to knowledgeable and enthusiastic audiences.

Live music can be found in bars and clubs several nights a week, when you might catch an established band with an international reputation or a new group testing the waters. Hotels will also lay on entertainment and are a frequent venue for steel pan music, folk dancing and mock carnival singing and dancing. You can also find invited artistes in drama, dance, cabaret and comedy who come for a week or so to put on a show or to take part in a festival.

Cinema

There is no home-grown film industry on Barbados, but you can find the latest Hollywood releases if you are stuck for something to do on a rainy day. A good range of films is shown, with plenty of choice for children as well as adults of all ages and tastes. The best place to go is the Multiplex at the Sheraton centre (see below), which is big enough to host events such as film festivals. Other cinemas have closed because of the competition from video clubs pirating films and releasing them at the same time as the film hits the cinemas.

Globe, Upper Roebuck St, by roundabout, Bridgetown, **T** 4264692. *US$4 for regular seats, US$5 for balcony. Map 3, G4, p219* New releases and older classics. You get two films for your admission fee.

Globe Drive In, Adams Castle, Christ Church, off the ABC Highway by the Sheraton Centre, **T** 4370479. *Turn off at Garfield Sobers roundabout. Usually US$4 for two films. Map 3, I7, p219* Sit under the stars to watch a movie. Same sort of selection as at the Globe.

Olympus Theatres Multiplex, Sheraton Centre, Christ Church, **T** 4371000, **T** 2285255 (room hire), www.olympustheatres.com. *Map 3, I6, p219* Stadium style seating for 1,633 with six screens, all digital sound, showing films starting every 15 minutes from 1400 onwards. Other facilities include the *Ambrosia Net Café* and *Ambrosia Jazz Café*, with Mexican food and brochetas, music, art displays and high-speed internet access. Puppet shows are planned and there are occasionally live musical performances. Rooms can be hired for children's birthday parties or conferences for adults (see above for phone number).

Dance

No visitor to Barbados can fail to notice the extent to which music and dance pervade daily life. Whether it is reggae pounding out from a passing ZR van or gospel music being belted out in a church, Bajan rhythm is inescapable. The West Africans, dragged to the island as slaves, brought with them tastes in music and dance which are still evident today. Bajans are born with the ability to gyrate their hips on the dance floor with energy, rhythm and sex appeal, a skill called 'wukkin up', which tourists spend many happy – though ultimately, unsuccessful – hours trying to emulate. This intensity of sound and beat has produced many musicians, several of which have become world famous, such as **The Mighty Gabby**, reggae vocalist and songwriter **David Kirton**, jazz saxophonist **Arturo Tappin**, **Red Plastic Bag and John King**, **Krosfyah**, **Square One** and **Spice** as well as the singer **Rihanna**, who burst onto the world scene in 2005 and shot straight up the charts, and the queen of soca, **Alison Hinds**, who left *Square One* in 2005 to go solo. See also Music, also p197.

Theatre

Despite the small size of the island and the neglect it suffered during colonial times, Barbados has a long tradition in the performing arts. There are records of 17th-century 'tea meetings' during which people recited poetry, speeches, Biblical passages or humorous stories, while troupes of actors toured the islands by ship and gave open air performances wherever they landed.

The Patagonian Theatre was built in 1783 but performances were designed for white colonial audiences with white actors until after the Second World War. At that time the **Green Room Players** were formed and they staged local and international multi-ethnic plays. The non-profit **Stage One Theatre Productions** was created in 1977, specializing in traditional plays to promote interest in drama. They also organize an annual Stage One Playwriting Contest. **WWB Productions** concentrates on workshops throughout the Caribbean, exploring indigenous materials and costumes and encouraging local talent. **Laff It Off** (www.laffitoff.com) is the leading comedy group, taking a satirical look at political and social issues and focussing on the activities of politicians, community leaders, sports and television personalities.

There are several good semi-professional theatre companies and cultural groups ranging from drama to church choirs. The list of theatre groups includes the aforementioned Green Room Players, Stage One Theatre Productions, WWB Productions and Laff It Off Productions, as well as the **St John Folk and Dramatic Group**, **Bajan Bus Stop**, **Pampalam** and the **Pinelands Creative Workshop**, which is also involved in dance. Other dance groups include **Dancing Africa**, **Dance National Afrique**, the **Barbados Dance Theatre Company** and **Dance Strides**.

1627 And All That, Barbados Museum, **T** 4281627, goldsands@ caribsurf.com. *Thu 1830-2200. Map 6, A8, p224* A humorous take on Barbados' history with a colourful show which has been going for years. US$62.50 including transport, tour of the museum, hors d'oeuvres, buffet dinner, complimentary bar, steel band show and craftmarket.

Daphne Joseph-Hackett Theatre, Queen's Park, **T** 4277267. *Performances usually start at 2000. Map 5, C12, p223* Named after a teacher who was instrumental in promoting theatre in Barbados and now the main theatre for drama and comedy.

! During George Washington's visit in 1751 he wrote in his diary about attending a theatrical performance, *The History of George Barnwell*, which appears to have spurred a lifelong interest in the theatre.

Frank Collymore Hall, in the Tom Adams Financial Centre, Bridgetown, www.fch.org.bb. *Map 5, C9, p223* Frank Appleton Collymore (1893-1980) was a poet, actor and teacher who devoted his life to developing the performing arts in Barbados. A bronze bust of 'Colly' by Karl Broodhagen stands at the entrance. This is the main venue for music, dance and drama but the 500-seat hall is also used for conferences and lectures and it fulfils an educational as well as cultural function. It opened in 1986 with a week of dance, gospel, calypso, folk, classical music and jazz, called 'City Nights'. Each year it hosts the NIFCA finals (see p147). Performances are advertised in the press. It is usually wise to buy tickets in advance. Most people dress quite formally for these performances.

Plantation Restaurant, St Lawrence, **T** 4285048. *Wed and Fri at 1830 prompt. The show finishes at 2230 but you can stay later for drinks. US$75 with buffet dinner and transport from hotel, US$47.50 without transport. Map 3, I7, p219* Hosts the *Bajan Roots and Rhythms Tropical Spectacular Dinner Show*, a cabaret show with scantily-clad dancers performing pseudo-traditional folk dances loosely based on the island's history and legends. It's purely for tourist consumption and is all good fun and slickly produced.

There is something going on nearly every month in Barbados: carnival celebrations, sporting fixtures, music and cultural festivals, something for everyone. The main carnival is Crop Over, which celebrates the end of the sugar cane harvest. For about 30 years it went uncelebrated because of The Second World War and subsequent economic difficulties, but was resurrected for tourist purposes in 1974. Since then it has grown into a major celebration of Bajan culture enjoyed by all and nobody gets much work done during the five weeks that it lasts: 'more than a carnival, sweet fuh days'. Many villages will also hold a 'street fair' from time to time. For a diary of events and festivals see www.barbados.org/eventcd.htm

January

Jazz Festival, a seven-day affair, sees the arrival of international and Barbadian musicians such as Chucho Valdés and Randy Crawford, to play in intensive jazz concerts. Held at several locations such as Garfield Sobers Auditorium, Heritage Park, Sunbury Plantation House and Farley Hill. Tickets from US$12.50. Contact Gilbert Rowe, **T** 4374537, www.barbadosjazzfestival.com.

Barbados Horticultural Society (BHS) Annual Flower Show, held on the last weekend at BHS Headquarters, Balls, Christ Church, **T** 4285889.

February

Holetown Festival commemorates the first settlers' landing at St James in February 1627. There are parades with floats during the day, all well-organized and restrained, nothing outrageous. The Mallalieu Motor Collection lends its vintage cars, one of which carries Miss Holetown; a military band parades behind three police horses, a few kids march in costume, there are one or two masked performers, but the event is hugely popular with crowds lining the street from Sunset Crest to the Post Office. Along the grass verge, stalls are set up, selling jewellery, food, T-shirts, wraps, toys, tat, art, and of course there are the ubiquitous rumshops and Banks beer. All do good business with tourists and locals alike. In the evening there are different events on offer. Don't miss the police band playing on stage at the edge of the beach. This is Little England par excellence. The audience sits on neat rows of chairs on the sand, politely listening, a very colonial image against the setting sun, until the band tries to sell its latest CD. There are other, more contemporary shows on different nights, but none goes on beyond 2200. Contact Alfred Pragnell, **T** 4356264.

Cream of the festival crop

Crop Over, held when the sugar cane harvest ends, is the island's main festival or carnival, with parades and calypso competitions over the weekend leading up to Kadooment Day (the first Monday in August), and calypso 'tents' for several weeks beforehand. Your eyes will be blasted with colour by costumed dancers, stilt walkers and masqueraders, your ears blasted with sound by tuk bands, calypso, ringbang and steel pan, and your head blasted by rum, beer, sun, adrenaline and lack of sleep. The celebrations begin with the ceremonial delivery of the last canes on a brightly-coloured dray cart pulled by mules, which are blessed. There is a toast to the sugar workers and the crowning of the King and Queen of the crop (the champion cutter-pilers). Weekly calypso tent shows showcase the latest songs with performances by entertainers and comedians as well as calypsonians (see p197). Parties, also known as fêtes or bashments, start with after work liming, hot up around midnight and go on until daybreak. Check with costume bands for their band fetes. The Junior Kadooment Parade and Junior Calypso Monarch Competition give children a chance to have their own carnival and play 'mas'. Things start to hot up big time with the Pic-O-De-Crop semi finals and Party Monarch Calypso competition. From a line up of 18, seven competitors are selected to go forward to the finals to compete against the reigning Calypso Monarch. This is now held on the East Coast

---

March

Holders Season, two weeks in mid March. This is the major music, opera, drama and cabaret festival in the Caribbean.

Road and combined with the Party Monarch Calypso competition, so a great day is had by all with picnics, music and liming overlooking the Atlantic surf. Following the selection of the King of Pic-O-De-Crop Calypso there is Fore-Day Morning Jump Up, an early morning event borrowed from Trinidad's carnival which has proved a great success. It starts in Bridgetown and heads out to Spring Garden (wear old clothes as a lot of oils and paints get liberally smeared around). Cohobblopot is when the kings and queens of the costume bands show off their creations and compete for prizes and the titles of King and Queen of the Festival. Kadooment is the grand finale of the carnival, when there is a procession of costume bands through the streets, accompanied by trucks of deafening sound systems and fuelled by alcohol. Membership of a band is not restricted to locals, anyone can join and there is a range of costumes to suit all figures and complexions. Three very popular bands are *Baje International*, www.baje-intl.com, *Power X 4*, www.power xfour.com and the *Refugees*, www.refugeescamp.com

Wear plenty of sun block and drink lots of water to keep yourself hydrated and compensate for the alcohol. For more information contact the **National Cultural Foundation**, T 4240909, www.barbados.org/cropover.

Another useful website is www.kadooment.com, which lists activities on a daily basis, and provides contact details for costume bands.

International artistes are invited to Barbados to perform in plays, opera, cabaret, musicals, classical or jazz concerts, folk music and recitals, in the spectacular outdoor setting of the garden of Holders House, owned by John and Wendy Kidd, beautifully situated just above the polo ground. When Pavarotti sang there a few years ago, the entire polo field was occupied by an eager audience, but a smaller audience for a more intimate show such as Kit and the Widow with Melanie Marshall in *When the Fat Lady Sings* can be accommodated around the swimming pool, while a stage is erected on the lawn for plays such as *The Complete Works of Shakespeare*, presented by the Reduced Shakespeare Company. Not all the talent is imported, however, and you can expect to see Bajan artists and choirs join forces with the visitors.

The 2006 season saw the première of *Redemption – The Musical*, a new musical by Barbadian Al Boots, set in the world of ballet. The international pianist, Joanna MacGregor performed and the main drama event was Shakespeare's *Romeo and Juliet*. The setting is unbelievably romantic, in the garden of Holders House, with thousands of fairy lights twinkling in the palm trees and among the shrubs. Take a picnic and a bottle of bubbly or Chardonnay, it's a great social occasion. Don't forget your umbrella and insect repellent. For details see **T** 4326385, www.holders.net.

April

Congaline Street Festival, held around Easter, with music, art and culture at de Congaline Village set up on the Dover playing field in St Lawrence Gap, finishing with a jump up in the streets from Garrison Savannah to Spring Garden. Bajan and other Caribbean music. Contact the National Cultural Foundation, **T** 4240909, ncf@caribsurf.com.

Oistins Fish Festival, held around Easter, celebrates the signing of the Charter of Barbados and the history of this fishing town. There are three days of competitions, parades, demonstrations of fishing skills such as fish boning, and a big street party with music which goes on until late at night – and of course, lots of fried fish and fish cakes. A very popular event which attracts thousands of people, while TV crews from the USA and Canada spread it to 40 million more. Contact Dan Carter, **T** 4286738.

May

Gospelfest, held over Whitsun, the last weekend in May, is an international festival attracting gospel singers from the USA, UK and all over the Caribbean. Contact Adrian Agard, **T** 4265940, www.barbadosgospelfest.com.

Celtic Festival is a rather unusual festival to be celebrated in the Caribbean, but it attracts Celtic people from around the world for their annual gymanfa-ganu and other events including sports, such as rugby and Highland Games on the beach, or traditional Scottish music, Welsh clog dancing and Appalachian music and dancing. It overlaps and is followed by the **International Folk Festival**, which runs into June. Contact Ruth Williams, **T** 4263387, celticruth@hotmail.com.

July/August

Crop Over is held over five weeks from mid-July (see box p144).

October

Blowin' in de Windies, a new youth jazz festival, attracts school bands from the UK, North and South America and the Caribbean, with performances and workshops. JazzMatazz night brings together music, dance and a fashion show. Contact Ruth Williams, **T** 4263387, celticruth@hotmail.com.

November

The National Independence Festival of Creative Arts (NIFCA), has been held annually since 1973. It opens in September and runs through October and November, with concerts, exhibitions of photography, art, craft, sculpture, pottery and the performing arts. Starting at community level, competitors work their way up through parish heats to reach the finals at the Frank Collymore Hall in Bridgetown, see p139. Contact The National Cultural Foundation, **T** 4240909, ncf@caribsurf.com.

Independence Day, although the actual day is 30 November, there are several events throughout the month commemorating Barbados' independence from Britain in 1966.

Shopping

Prices are generally high, but the range of goods available is excellent. Food is not cheap but most things are available and good quality. For those who are self-catering, or just looking for picnic material, the supermarkets on the west and south coasts are excellent and several of them organize transport for shopping trips or will deliver if you order online. Fresh fruit and vegetables usually come from Trinidad, Venezuela or other neighbouring countries. There is a good selection in the supermarkets or there are market stalls dotted around the island selling at similar prices. Street vendors are very persistent but generally friendly even when you refuse their wares. Fish can be bought fresh from the fish market at Oistins or from the fishermen where they land their catch, such as at Six Men's Bay, north of Port St Charles, Speightstown. Rum, beer, wine and other alcoholic beverages are cheapest in the supermarkets where there is a wide choice with frequent special offers,. However, for a better, or more upmarket, selection try Wine World in Rockley and on the Spring Garden Highway (see p155).

Art galleries

Barbados Arts Council, at the Pelican Craft Village, **T** 4264385. *Daily 0900-2130. Map 5, C1, p222* Also at The Coach House, St James. The Barbados Arts Council is a non-profit organization set up to foster Barbadian art and artists. Works exhibited at these galleries are drawn from its 300 members. Those shown are by established artists with an international reputation to those just starting out. There are also prints for sale.

Beyond Aesthetics Gallery, 34 Regency Park, Christ Church, **T** 2280485. *Map 3, H6, p218* Barbadian art by John WF Walcott and floral creations by Mary Walcott.

Freedom Fine Art Gallery, Shop 4a, Chattel Village, Holetown, **T** 4327047. *Map 2, L2, p217* Regional and local art, limited selection but growing, also prints.

Gallery of Caribbean Art, Northern Business Centre, Speightstown, St Peter, **T** 4190858, www.artgallerycaribbean.com. *Mon-Fri 0930-1630, Sat 0930-1400. Map 2, G1, p217* A gallery which exhibits work from Barbados, the Caribbean and elsewhere. Large collection of paintings which can be shipped abroad for you.

The Gallery St James, 2nd St, Holetown, **T** 4322789. *Map 2, L2, p217* Caribbean and international art, private collection of antiquarian maps, jazz paintings of Marsha Hammel and work of Trinidadian artist, Boscoe Holder.

Gang of 4 Art Studio, Speightstown, **T** 4190051. *Map 2, G1, p217* Art and sculpture in the home studio of Gordon Webster with additional works by Lilian Sten, Aziza and Ras Bongo Congo-I.

Mango's Fine Art Gallery, Mango's Restaurant (see p120), West End 2 Queen St, Speightstown, St Peter, **T** 4220704, www.mangosart.com. *Open evenings or by appointment. Map 2, G1, p217* A retrospective of Michael Adams' paintings and silk screen prints with exceptional use of colour and concentrating on jungle scenes, rain forest and waterfalls.

On the Wall, The Tides Restaurant (see p121), Holetown, St James, **T** 4248329, and at Earthworks Pottery (see p154), **T** 4389246, www.onthewallgallery.com. *Mon-Fri 0800-2200, Sat-Sun 1600-2200. Map 2, L1, p217* Local and regional works of art are exhibited on the walls of the bar, courtyard and reception areas of the restaurant. Shipping service available.

Verandah Art Gallery, Old Spirit Bond Mall, overlooking the Careenage, Bridgetown, **T** 4262605. *Mon-Fri 0900-1630, Sat 0930-1400. Map 5, E7, p223* Has a wide selection with some Haitian and Cuban art, as well as other contemporary Caribbean paintings, carvings and batik, and temporary exhibitions.

Zemicon Gallery, James Fort Building, Hicks St, Bridgetown, **T** 4300054. *Tue-Fri 1000-1600 or by appointment. Map 5, E6, p222* Shows some of the best local artists. It is making a statement by being bold and contemporary.

Bookshops

The Book Place, Probyn St, Bridgetown. *Mon-Sat 0900-1700. Map 5, F9, p223* Specializes in Caribbean material and has a good secondhand section.

The Cloister, Hicks St, Bridgetown, **T** 4262662. *Mon-Sat 0900-1700. Map 5, E6, p222* Probably has the largest stock with a good range of Caribbean material and sells *Footprint Handbooks*.

Talking shop

There is lots of well-advertised duty-free shopping and many jewellery shops such as Diamonds International and Colombian Emeralds. Visitors who produce their passport and air ticket can take most duty-free goods away from the store for use in the island before they leave (but not camera film or alcohol). Cameras and electrical goods may be cheaper in an ordinary discount store in the USA or Europe than duty free in Barbados. Travellers who are going on to other islands may find it useful to do some shopping here. If coming from another Caribbean island there are strict controls on bringing in fresh fruit and vegetables. If you want to buy more Barbadian produce and souvenirs once you get home, try www.shopinbarbados.com, a US-based website listing food, music, crafts, books, art, games and gifts.

The Pages Bookstore, at Cave Shepherd, Broad St and West Coast Mall. *Mon-Sat 0900-1700. Map 5, D7, p223* Also has a reasonable selection. If you shop online from Super Centre supermarket you can buy books from the Pages Bookstore with your groceries.

Crafts

Best of Barbados, Mall 34 on Broad St in Bridgetown *Map 5, D7, p223* Chattel Village in Holetown, Southern Palms and *Walkers' World* in St Lawrence Gap, Quayside Centre in Hastings, *Orchid World* and the Bridgetown Cruise Terminal, www.best-of-barbados.com. The ultimate gift shop with every Barbados souvenir imaginable. The designs mostly stem from the work of Jill Walker, who has been living and painting in Barbados since 1955, and they have a network

> ### The monkey jar
>
> A monkey jar is a traditional vessel for storing drinking water and keeping it cool in the days before fridges. Known as a 'monkey' it is made from local terracotta clay and fired to 1100°C. The clay is slightly porous, allowing some of the water to penetrate it and make the exterior very cold, which in turn keeps the water inside cool. It looks more like a teapot than a monkey or a jar, but some potters decorate and customize the jar with monkey attributes for the tourist market.

of cottage workers making things exclusively for the shop. Her prints of local scenes are on sale, mugs, candles and T-shirts. *Walkers' World* sells furniture and home accessories as well as gifts and has a café overlooking Dover Beach.

Earthworks Pottery, Edgehill Heights No 2, St Thomas, **T** 4250223, www.earthworks-pottery.com. *Mon-Fri 0900-1700, Sat 0900-1300. Map 3, C4, p218* The best place to come for local pottery you can actually use: solid houseware and pots in blues and greens with several different designs, mix and match square, round and rectangular dishwasher safe crockery. They will also make commissioned pieces. VAT-free for visitors. On the premises there is also a small restaurant/café, *The Tree House*, see p125, where you can see the plates and bowls in use, a batique shop and a gift shop with crafts from several local artists.

Pelican Craft Centre, Princess Alice Highway, near the harbour, **T** 4275350, bidc@bidc.org. *Mon-Fri 0900-1800, Sat 0900-1400. Map 5, C1, p222* This may look like a tourist trap, designed to ensnare cruise ship passengers, but the great thing about it is that all the crafts are made in Barbados and you can even watch the artisans at work in the 25 shops and workshops. Designed to look like chattel houses, the craft centre has batik, carvings, paintings, pottery, jewellery, glass, metal work and lots of other handicrafts.

Red Clay Pottery, Fairfield Cross Rd, St Michael, **T** 4243800, redclay@su⋯ ⋯00-1300. *Map 3, F3, p218* F⋯ ceramic art, dishwashe⋯ glazes are lead free. The p⋯ wo miles from Bridgetow⋯ d tour.

Highland Pottery

Departm⋯

Cave Sh⋯ ⋯ West Coast Mall at Sunset ⋯ Shepherd Plaza, Holetown ⋯ ⋯e island. It offers a shoppin⋯ ⋯tels on the south and west coasts; **I** 4312078 between ⋯ ⋯ for customer service, or hop on a local bus, B\$1.50.

Food and drink

Gourmet Shop, Chattel Village, Holetown, **T** 4327711, thegourmetshop@caribsurf.com. *Mon-Sat 0900-1800, 1000-1400 holidays and festivals. Map 3, B2, p218* Excellent selection of luxury food and wine for a special treat or if you are missing something from home.

Patisserie Flindt, Holetown and Hastings, **T** 4322626/4352600, www.flindtbarbados.com. *Map 2, L2, p217* and *Map 3, I4, p218* Chocolate cakes, sweet temptations, also canapés, picnic boxes and desserts. Now diversifying with **Bistro Flindt on the Hill** at Sugar Hill Resort, St James, **T** 4197622.

Wine World, Spring Garden Highway, St Michael, **T** 2280193
Map 3, I5, p219, and Rockley Main Rd, Christ Church, **T** 4358523,
info@wineworldinc.com. *Map 3, F2, p218 Mon-Fri 0900-1800, Sat
0900-1300*. Fine wines, rum and other spirits from around the world.
Not cheap, but good selection. They sometimes hold tastings and
offer a party service with all soft drinks and accessories.

Shopping malls

West Coast Mall, Holetown. *Map 3, B2, p218* With supermarket,
bank, pharmacy, travel agent, internet access, and a Chattel Village
beside it with boutiques, cafés and the Gourmet Shop.

On the south coast there are three small malls, all within half
a mile of each other in Hastings and Worthing: **Hastings Plaza**,
Quayside Centre and **Shak Shak Complex**.

Sheraton Centre, off the ABC Highway in Christ Church.
Map 3, I6, p219 Less touristy and designed for the local market.
Air-conditioned mall with 70 stores, a food court and cinema
complex.

Supermarkets

JBs Mastermart, Wildey. *Mon-Tue 0800-1900, Wed-Sat 0800-
2000, Sun 0900-1300. Map 3, H5, p219* The best stocked of all.
Big B, 200 yds from the Rendezvous turning, Worthing. *Mon-Tue
0800-1900, Wed-Sat 0800-2000, Sun 0900-1300 Map 3, J5, p219*
Easy to reach by public transport. Photocopying available. **Super
Centre**, five stores including Oistins and Holetown,
www.supercentre.com. *Mon-Tue 0800-1900, Wed-Sat 0800-2000,
Sun 0900-1300 Map 3, J8, p219 and B2, p218* Will take orders on
internet and deliver, no delivery charge, minimum order B$50.
Payment by credit card. Orders also by fax.

The people of Barbados are sport mad and the facilities for pursuing a sport of your choice are excellent for an island of this size. Cricket still draws the largest following and there are dozens of famous cricketers who are household names. Going to watch a cricket match is an entertaining cultural experience and well worth doing, even if you don't understand the game. Football and rugby are also played and followed enthusiastically by the crowd. An unusual spectator sport for a Caribbean island is horse racing, which is exciting to watch, but even more extraordinary is polo, which appears to have been imported wholesale from the Home Counties and is followed avidly by mostly white Barbadians and ex-pats. Participation sports are also well-developed and there are great facilities for visitors to play golf, tennis and several other sports. The sea is a natural water playground and you can scuba dive, sail, fish, windsurf, kitesurf and body surf as well as hire more low-key water toys on the beach.

Contact the **National Sports Council**, Blenheim, St Michael,
T 4366127, for information on any sport not mentioned here
or pick up the annual brochure, *Sporting Barbados*,
www.sportingbarbados.com.

Athletics

Sir Garfield Sobers Sports Complex, Wildey, St Michael,
T 4376016. *Map 3, H6, p219* A multi-purpose gymnasium offering
badminton, bodybuilding, boxing, basketball, gymnastics,
handball, judo, karate, netball, table tennis, volleyball and
weightlifting. There are plenty of changing rooms and showers
and also sauna and massage rooms, a medical room and
warm-up/practice area.

Badminton

Community College, St Michael. Played on Tuesdays at 1930
and Saturdays at 1300. Equipment available. **Barbados
Badminton Association**, Ansley Edey, **T** 4188000.

Cricket

Cricket is King in Barbados and everybody has an opinion on the
state of the game as well as the latest results. There is lots of village
cricket all over the island at weekends. A match here is nothing if
not a social occasion. Great Bajan cricketers become icons and five
have been knighted for their services to the game and their
country: Sir Garfield Sobers (the only living National Hero), Sir

! It is alleged that the Empire Cricket Club at Bank Hall
● loved fast wickets so much that they rubbed soap into the
wicket. This gave a fast bowler an extra yard of pace but
caused many a batsman to take a tumble.

Cricket in the Caribbean

Test matches in the Caribbean are played in Jamaica, Barbados, Guyana, St Kitts, St Lucia, Trinidad and Antigua. In 2006 the West Indies hosted Zimbabwe and India for Test Matches, but none were held in Barbados because of rebuilding works at the Kensington Oval. St Kitts is being used instead for the first time. Other first-class and one-day matches may be played in some of the smaller islands, part of either the Windward Islands or Leeward Islands teams, such as Grenada, Dominica, St Vincent, Montserrat or Anguilla. The six first-class teams are: Jamaica, Trinidad and Tobago, Barbados, Guyana, Windward Islands and Leeward Islands. Antigua is hoping to play separately from the Leeward Islands at some time in the future.

Relaxed entertainment on a huge scale can also be enjoyed by going to inter-island matches. Currently the one-day competition is being played before Christmas; the four-day competition runs from January to March. Unless West Indies are on tour at the time all the international players are required to play in the competition, so the standard is high. A new regional tournament starts in August /September 2006, devised to regenerate cricket in the Caribbean. Financed by Allen Stanford (owner of Caribbean Star airline and the Sticky Wicket cricket ground in Antigua), who is funding training and coaching as well

Conrad Hunte, Sir Everton Weekes, Sir Clyde Walcott and Sir Frank Worrell. In addition to Test Matches and inter-island competitions there are tournaments for the young and old: the Sir Garfield Sobers International Schools Tournament and the Sir Garfield Sobers Seniors Cricket Festival being two of the most important. Barbados is the premier cricket tour destination in the world and as the competition itself, 17 countries will compete in the Twenty20 tournament: Anguilla, Antigua and Barbuda, Bahamas, Barbados, Bermuda, Cayman Islands, Dominica, Grenada, Guyana, Jamaica, Montserrat, St Kitts and Nevis, St Lucia, Sint Maarten, British Virgin Islands, St Vincent, Trinidad and Tobago. Stanford also plans to set up a professional Super League in the region and stage two games in November 2006 featuring a Caribbean Super Stars XI against an international team.

Women's cricket is also popular in the West Indies and the team came fifth in the 2005 International Women's Cricket Council World Cup held in South Africa.

Information about international matches can be obtained in the UK from the **England and Wales Cricket Board (ECB)**, Lord's Cricket Ground, St John's Wood, London NW8 8QN, T020-74321200. However, finding out about the first-class matches between the islands is more difficult and best one on the internet.

Some useful websites for news, scores and statistics: www.caribbeancricket.com, www.windiescricket.com and www.uk.cricinfo.com. Tickets for the Digicel Test Series held in the Caribbean can be purchased by calling toll free from within the Caribbean, the West Indies ticket line T 1-800-744-GAME, or from outside the region T 1-268-481-2490.

cricket lovers, or indeed fans of great sporting and social occasions, should try to arrange their visit to coincide with a Test Match or a One Day International at the new Kensington Oval, to be completed in 2006. Crowd participation is an education to anyone who has never experienced a West Indian audience and the atmosphere is electric. No sedate Sunday afternoon crowd this –

2007 Cricket World Cup

The 2007 Cricket World Cup is to be held in the West Indies, the third biggest sporting event in the world after the Olympics and Fifa football. Thousands of spectators are expected to travel to the region while some 2 billion will watch the event on television. Work is being done to upgrade cricket facilities in traditional, yet out-of-date, venues, as well as expand and renovate hotel accommodation. The final is to be held in Barbados, where the Kensington Oval stands are being demolished and rebuilt with the same names but offering better facilities including high quality hospitality suites and access for the disabled. With temporary stands, total capacity will be 27,000, dropping to 15,000 after the World Cup. There will be media facilities for 800 journalists, who will all be wanting broadband, cellular phones and other connections to the world outside. In Antigua and Guyana new grounds are to be built: the Sir Vivian Richards stadium and the Providence stadium, while upgrades are planned for Queen's Park, Grenada, Sabina Park, Jamaica, Queens Park Oval, Trinidad and Tobago, Beausejour Stadium, St Lucia, and a complete renovation and upgrade at Warner Park Stadium, St Kitts and Nevis, see www.icc-cricket.com/events/worldcup/venues.html For dates of matches and how to get tickets, see www.cricketworldcup.com and for news and comment try the unofficial www.worldcupweb.com.

the DJ pounds out the music, there is constant whistling, horn-blowing, cheering and banter, public announcements and ribald entertainment from cal#ypsonian, MacFingall, in the Kensington Stand. Everything stops for a Test Match and the offices are empty of workers, who are 'in meetings' all day. The biggest crowds come for the matches against England, with touring teams tagging along, but cricket tourists come from as far as Australia or South Africa. For information about the bigger matches at Kensington Oval or arranging matches against local teams, contact **Barbados Cricket Association**, **T** 4361397, www.cwcricket.com. If you and your local team want to tour Barbados, **Sporting Barbados**, **T** 2289122, www.sporting barbados.com, will help with discounts and keeping the costs down or to put you in touch with a specialist tour agency.

Chess, draughts, dominoes and warri

Chess, draughts (checkers in the USA), dominoes and warri are played to a high standard. Join a rumshop match at your peril. Even the Prime Minister is a keen **dominoes** player. The best 'slammers' compete in a league and the national team has won the world championship several times. Barbados has a world champion **draughts** player, Suki King. The island's Sports Person of the Year 2001 was the first Barbadian **chess** player to reach the rank of International Master, 34 year old Kevin Denny. **Warri** is a board game which has been around since time immemorial and has been traced to the ancient Kush civilizations on the Upper Nile. It is believed to have come over to the Caribbean with the slaves. For more information contact Lee Farnum-Badley, **T** 4321292, badley@mail.sunbeach.net.

Cycling

Cycling is best on the east coast, but traffic is dangerously heavy everywhere else and rush hour from 1600 makes cycling unpleasant in built up areas.

Contact the **Mountain Bike Association**, Wayne Robinson, **T** 4310419, or Robert Quintyne, **T** 4293367.

Flex Bicycle Rentals, **T** 2311518 (mob), **T** 4240321, gmgriff@sunbeach.net. Run by Paul Griffith. Bike hire US$15. Tours on Fridays and Saturdays.

Odyssey Tours, **T** 2280003, odyssey@inaccessbb.com. Offer ecological and historical excursions by bike.

Fishing

Charter boats for game fishing are lined up along the Careenage, so you can inspect the goods before making a decision on who to call.

Fishing Charters Barbados, **T** 4292326, www.bluemarlin barbados.com. Arrange deep-sea day or night fishing trips on the *Blue Marlin*, *Idyll Time* and *Blue Jay*. Others include *Honey Bea III*, **T** 4285344, honeybea111@hotmail.com.

The Barbados Game Fishing Association, 230 Atlantic Shores, Christ Church, **T** 4286668, www.barbadosgamefishing.com. Runs an international tournament from February to April. The targets are blue marlin, yellow fin tuna, white marlin, sailfish, wahoo and dolphin (mahi mahi). The record catch on rod and reel is held by Graham Manning, who landed a 910-lb blue marlin in 1996. Dave Marshall is the Secretary.

Football

The Barbados national team is the Rockets and they play international matches at the National Stadium. Although they are ranked in the top 100 teams in the world, they have yet to qualify for the World Cup. The best players play professionally in the UK and Ireland as football is essentially amateur in Barbados. Touring teams are welcome, from school sides to veterans. There are many football pitches around the island, some of which are floodlit. The biggest annual event is the International Masters Football Festival at the end of May, which attracts teams from the Caribbean and the UK. Contact Paul Wright, **T** 4281128, pwright@sunbeach.net, or the **Barbados Football Association**, **T** 2281707, barbadosfootball@hotmail.com.

Golf

Many keen golfers come here just to play golf and there are enough courses to keep anyone busy for a while. New courses will soon be opened at Apes Hill, St James and at Sugar Hill, St Joseph. The Barbados Open Golf Championship is held in November and the Senior PGA European Golf Tournament in March. The Sir Garry Sobers Festival of Golf in April is played on three courses with 240 players including former Test cricketers, celebrities and professional golfers.

Sandy Lane, **T** 4322946. *Map 2, B2, p217* There are other championship courses but this is the best and most prestigious. There are two Tom Fazio 18-hole courses, Country Club and the Green Monkey (where Tiger Woods got married), and a nine-hole course, the Old Nine, all on 600 acres of former sugar cane land next to the hotel (see p105).

Royal Westmoreland Golf and Country Club, St James, **T** 4224653. *Map 2, J2-3, p217* An 18-hole, par 72, Robert Trent Jones Jr course and another nine-hole one spread over 480 acres on a hilly site in St James with views over the west coast. To play here you must be staying in one of the villas or at a hotel with an access agreement. Members can use the hotel's beach club facilities a five-minute drive away. Construction of 350 villas around one of the nine-hole loops has now started, three club houses, a swimming pool and five tennis courts.

Barbados Golf Club, Durants, Christ Church, **T** 4288463, www.barbadosgolfclub.com. *Map 3, I8, p219* Open to the public, 18-hole Championship golf course, 6,700 yards, par 72 and an official destination of the PGA European tour. Green fees are US$120 in high season, US$80 in low season. Also tuition, three- and seven-day passes, duty-free pro shop, club and shoe rentals. Packages can be arranged with partner hotels.

Almond Beach Village, next to the Heywoods course in the northwest, **T** 4224900. *Map 2, G1, p217* A nine-hole course.

Ocean Park, at Balls in Christ Church, **T** 4207405. *0900-1800, US$20, children US$12.50. Map 4, L1, p221* 18-hole mini course (fun for families, not serious golfers). Attached to Ocean Park, a new aquarium, included in the price, see p43. Snack bar, gift shop, outdoor chess and draughts.

Hockey

Hockey is played on an astroturf hockey pitch at the Sir Garfield Sobers Sports Complex. There are also matches at the Kensington Oval cricket ground (to be resumed after the Cricket World Cup in 2007) and Wildey Astroturf. Banks International Hockey Festival is the largest event of its type in the Americas and is held over a week in August with 37 local teams and some 26 from overseas including mixed hockey teams. Other hockey events are arranged around this time for touring sides. Contact the **Barbados Hockey Federation**, **T** 4235442, bhf@cariaccess.com.

Horse racing

The Barbados Turf Club, **T** 4263980, www.barbados turfclub.com. Holds flat race meetings at the Garrison on Saturdays during three seasons (January to March, May to October and

Obadele Thompson created Bajan history on 23 September 2000 when he won the first ever Olympic medal for his country. With a time of 10.04 seconds the 24 year old Oba won bronze in the Men's 100 m Final in Sydney. The name Obadele means 'the king comes home' and on his return to Barbados that was just how he was treated. Thousands lined the road from the airport to Bridgetown to welcome him home in royal fashion as a conquering hero and the Prime Minister conferred on him the title of 'Ambassador and special envoy to the youth of Barbados', effectively making him a diplomat. The honour brought with it certain mercenary benefits too as local businesses fell over themselves to be associated with him and Oba soon became the proud owner of a silver sports BMW convertible, a life insurance policy, free travel, accommodation at a top resort and a plot of land in the grand new housing development appropriately named Millennium Heights. At the 2004 Games in Athens, Oba made it to the final of the 100 m but didn't make it into the medals.

November to December). The biggest one being the Sandy Lane Gold cup held in March, which features horses from neighbouring islands. This is something of a social occasion, with parties, parades and concerts. The Royal Barbados Mounted Police band leads a parade of dancers, tumblers and stiltmen in carnival fashion and calypsonian Mac Fingall whips up the crowd with his own brand of fun, as he does at cricket matches. Horse racing dates back to colonial days when planters challenged each other to races. Later the cavalry officers of the British army joined in and by 1840 there were regular race days at the Garrison. If you can't get to a race meet you can watch training sessions at the

Sports

Garrison just after 0600 when the weather is still cool. Races are held in the heat of the day from 1330. Admission to the grandstand is US$5 but you can get a good view from various points around the track where there are betting shops and food stalls. The track is just under a mile long, oval shaped with a two-furlong finishing straight.

Polo

Polo has been played since cavalry officers introduced the game in the 19th century and the Polo Club was formed in 1884. There are now four polo fields on Barbados, with three new ones joining the long-established Holders Hill field in st James, where national and international matches are played between November and May. The sport used to be played at the Garrison, where ponies were often reject race horses, but in 1965 it moved to Holders Hill and its popularity has steadily risen since then.

Barbados Polo Club, Holders Hill, St James, **T** 4321080. *Map 3, C2, p219* Owned by the Kidd family, who also host Holders Season. Beautiful location, clubhouse for drinks, tea and cakes. US$7.50 entrance, US$2.50 tea and cakes.

Clifton Equestrian Centre, St Thomas, **T** 2312444. *Map 2, L7, p217* Owned by Bruce Bayley, a leading light in the sport of polo. Set among cane fields with panoramic views, it hosted the inaugural Barbados Open and caters for visiting players as well as beginners.

Lion Castle Polo Estate, St Thomas. *Map 2, L5, p217* Opened in 2005, 1,000 ft above sea level, as part of a luxury housing development on 64 acres with wonderful views to the south and east coasts.

Waterhall Polo Stables and Polo Field, Apes Hill, St James.
Map 2, J4, p217 Ponies for hire and training facilities for beginners.
Host to many top visiting teams, lovely location with ocean views.

Riding

There are many riding schools offering beach and/or country rides.
Some do not give instruction and cater for pleasure riding only.
Congo Road Equestrian Centre, T 4238293, Roberta Forster
provides a one-hour ride including lift to and from hotel for US$25,
beginners or advanced. **Brighton Stables**, on the west coast,
T 4259381. **Beau Geste Stables**, St George, T 4290139, Alison
Cox. **Tony's Riding School**, St Peter, T 4221549. **Caribbean
International Riding Centre**, St Joseph, Niaomi Roachford,
T 4227433, caribintriding@caribsur.com, good for trail riding,
US$60 for 1½ hours, US$82.50 for 2½ hours. **Trevena Riding
Stables**, St James, T 4326404. **Big C Riding Stables**, Christ
Church, T 4374056, contact Di Clarke, dineil@sunbeach.net.
Barbados Equestrian Association, Jenny Wilson, T 2289144,
jengi@sunbeach.net. Dressage events organized by the
Association are all held at Congo Road, near Six Roads, St Phillip.
For information, contact Jean Ray, T 4326404.

Road tennis

This is a an indigenous game dating from the 1930s, with defined
rules, played with a low wooden 'net' on some minor (and some
main) roads, car parks and school playgrounds. It is rather like a cross
between tennis and table tennis, played with wooden bats and a
skinned tennis ball, but scored like table tennis with most matches
being the best of five games. The most prestigious tournament is the
Racquets of Fire Road Tennis Championship held in October. For
information contact the **Professional Road Tennis Association
(PRTA)**, Dale Clarke, T 2338268, www.proroadtennis.com.

Rugby

There are three clubs playing rugby on Barbados and you can watch them at the Garrison. They welcome touring sides. They also play beach rugby by the *Carib Beach Bar* , see p130, on Sundays and other tournaments as part of the Celtic Festival in May, see p147. Contact Joe Whipple, **T** 4231380, whipple@sunbeach.net.

Running

Running has become more popular in Barbados since sprinter Obadele Thompson won an Olympic bronze medal and hurdler Andrea Blackett won gold at the Commonwealth Games, see box p167. All levels of fitness enthusiasts practice early morning at the Garrison. The Run Barbados Series is held in early December and comprises four races: a 10-km race, a half marathon, a marathon and a 4-km walk. This has proved so popular that entries rose from 300 in 1999 to 800 in 2000 and they are still rising into the thousands as everyone enjoys the carnival atmosphere. Contact Morris Greenidge at the **Barbados Tourism Authority**, **T** 4272623. Less ambitious are the trusty Hash Harriers with a run or walk of one to two hours on Saturdays, followed by a barbecue and drinks. For more details, **T** 4208113, www.barbadoshash.com.

Sailing

Barbados Yacht Club, Carlisle Bay, **T** 4271125. *Map 3, I3, p219* Holds regattas and offers sailing courses. Sailing can be a bit choppy along the south coast to Oistins and most races head up the west coast where the waters are calmer. The three-day Annual Mount Gay Rum Boatyard Regatta in May is the main event of the year. Carlisle Bay is the main anchorage and focal point for the sailing fraternity.

Scuba diving

Although Barbados is among the more developed islands in the Caribbean, reef life is not as bad as might be expected and some reefs are thriving although others are suffering from bleaching. Within the last few years the island has become known as a wreck diving destination. Five shipwrecks have been intentionally sunk as diving sites, offering interesting underwater photography, in addition to the many ships which have sunk in storms or battles during the life of this seafaring nation. Barbados is surrounded by an inner reef and an outer barrier reef. On the west coast the inner reef is within swimming distance for snorkelling or learning to dive, while the outer reef is a short boat ride away and the water is deeper. Here you can see barracuda, king fish, moray eels, turtles and squid as well as some fine black coral, barrel sponges and sea fans. Note that most dive shops and cruise boats hand feed turtles to make them tame and available. The underwater landscape may not be as pristine as some other islands, but there are some excellent wrecks worth exploring and Carlisle Bay is littered with bottles, cannon balls, anchors and small items such as buckles and buttons after many centuries of visiting ships 'losing' things overboard or sinking. There are 200 reported wrecks in Carlisle Bay, but another popular dive site is the *Stavronikita* in the Folkestone Marine Park, one of the best diving wrecks in the Caribbean. There are around 30 dive companies offering PADI diving courses, equipment rental and other facilities such as snorkelling.

Barbados Sub Aqua Club, at the *Boatyard Pub* on the waterfront on Bay St, Bridgetown, **T** 4216020 (Rob Bates). *Map 5, H10, p223* A branch of the British Sub Aqua Club (BSAC), they meet at 0800 on Sundays; they do not hire out equipment but if you have your own they are most welcoming to members from other branches.

Carib Ocean Divers, Royal Pavilion, **T** 4224414. *Map 2, J1, p217* Good, 32-ft boat with shower, dive platform and ladder, oxygen on board. Two-tank dive US$92, single tank US$52, beginners course US$92, Open Water Certification US$432, PADI and NAUI staff, good with beginners.

Dive Blue Reef, Mount Standfast, St James, **T** 4223133. *0800-1700. Map 2, J2, p217* Only six divers taken out on their 30-ft pirogue. Underwater camera rental.

Dive Shop Ltd, Aquatic Gap, St Michael, **T** 4269947, www.divebds.com. *Sun-Fri 0830-1630. Map 3, I3, p219* Two 30-ft boats taking 16 and 12 divers. Underwater camera rental. Good wreck diving close by. Sunday to Friday

Diving Adventures Barbados, Royal Mail Building, Cavans Lane, Bridgetown, **T** 4377445, divingbarbados@scubadiving.com. *Map 5, E7, p223* Daily single and two-tank dives, courses in English, German, Italian and Swedish.

Eastern Caribbean Safe Diving Association, Box 86 WRD, Welches Post Office. They help to maintain a recompression chamber at St Ann's Fort, **T** 4278819, for the Leeward and Windward Islands. It is attempting to establish minimum safe operating standards for dive shops, initially in the Eastern Caribbean and eventually, regionally.

Hightide Watersports, Coral Reef Club, St James, **T/F** 4320931, and at other locations such as Tamarind Cove, hightide@ sunbeach.net. *0830-1700*. Small groups of no more than eight.

Roger's Scuba Shack, at the Boatyard, Bridgetown, **T** 4363483, www.rogers-scubashack.com. *Map 5, H11, p223* A two-tank dive is US$85 plus 15% VAT, while snorkelling trips are offered for US$15. Lots of courses available, from Discover Scuba to Wreck Diver.

Underwater Barbados, Coconut Court Hotel, Hastings, or Carlisle Bay Centre, Bay St, St Michael, **T/F** 4260655. *Map 3, I4, p219*.

West Side Scuba Centre, Baku Beach, Holetown, **T/F** 4322558, www.westsidescuba.com. *Map 3, B1, p218* Two boats, small groups, certification and speciality courses available, dive packages and accommodation offered. US$92 for a two-tank dive, US$34.50 for a snorkelling boat trip and equipment rental. In the summer they dive the east coast where you can see larger fish and different underwater terrain.

Squash

There are squash courts at the Rockley Resort, **T** 4357880, **Barbados Squash Club**, Hastings, **T** 4277193 and the Casuarina Hotel, **T** 4283600. There is a local squash league and top players compete at a regional level in the Caribbean. For information contact the **Barbados Squash Racquets Association**, Chris Skinner, **T** 2284926.

Surfing

The best surfing is on the east coast at the Soup Bowl, Bathsheba, which has the most consistent break. The best time is August to November when you get perfect barrelling waves. Experienced surfers also like Duppies on the north coast, where you have a long paddle out and there is a lot of current, but the waves are really big. The south coast is good for beginners and for boogie boarding, and there is a good break at Brandons, while the west coast has some good spots with good access, often best when there are no waves on the east coast. Sandy Lane, Tropicana, Gibbs and Maycocks are all worth trying. The Barbados International Surfing Championship is held at the Soup Bowl, Bathsheba, in late November. **Barbados Surfing Association**, T 4265837 (Roger Miller). Equipment can be hired from **Irie Man**, T 4282866, www.irieman-talma.com (see also Windsurfing, p172) while Alan Burke runs a surf school at Long Beach catering for all ages and all levels, T 2285117, www.surfbarbados.tv.

Swimming

Aquatic Centre, adjacent to the Sir Garfield Sobers Sports Complex, T 4297946. *Map 3, H6, p219* Ten-lane Olympic-size swimming pool, tennis courts, hockey, football and cricket pitches outside.

Tennis

Nearly all the major hotels have tennis courts and many are lit for night play. Throughout the island there is a combination of public and private tennis facilities and some top class professional coaches providing tuition. The Sir Garfield Sobers Sports Complex (see p159) is the official home of the National Tennis Centre, but the other main centres are at Club Rockley Resort and the West Side Tennis Centre at Sunset Crest behind the Chattel House Village. A David and John Lloyd Tennis Village, www.sugarhillbarbados.com, has been built at Sugar Hill, in a

! The first 'citizen' of Sugar Hill was Cliff Richard, a keen tennis player who has generously allowed his property to be used as a holiday home by the rich and famous, most notably Prime Minister Tony Blair and his family.

prestigious development which includes condos and townhouses as well as a central clubhouse, world class tennis club, pool, fitness centre, restaurant and bar. The main court has lots of seating for spectators; there will be some tennis celebrity matches and visits from leading world players which will raise the profile of the game in Barbados. For information on the sport, contact **Barbados Lawn Tennis Association**, Ellie Brown, **T** 4302400.

Water Polo

Aquatic Centre, contact Stephen Lewis, **T** 4296767 (work), **T** 4286042 (home). Visitors are welcome to join in practice sessions with the team, which is sponsored by Banks beer. Training is on Mondays and Wednesdays at 1830, while matches are played on Saturdays at 1400.

Windsurfing and kitesurfing

The south coast is best for windsurfing. The centre of the action is Silver Rock, where Brian Talma, 'Irie Man', runs the windsurfing shop, **T** 4282866, www.irieman-talma.com. There is a two-mile stretch of reef providing excellent waves for wave sailors and a lagoon for those who are less confident. The best place to learn to windsurf is in the Sandy Beach area inside the lagoon, while outside the reef you can sometimes get good wave sailing. The most action can be found on the north coast, where Irie Man himself likes to go, to Cow Pens and Red Backs. Access is not easy and there is only a very small beach from which to launch yourself, but the waves can be very big. The International Funboard Challenge is held in March and the Barbados Windsurfing World Cup is in January. The Waterman Festival, held in late January and early February, is a professional international event where you can see lots of acrobatics. Contact the **Barbados Windsurfing Association**, at Silver Sands, **T** 4287277. *Map 4, L1, p221.*

Kitesurfing is best done further east near the airport, at Long Beach, where the wind is side on shore. The wind is best from November to July. When the wind is light and windsurfers can't go out, then the area between Silver Sands Resort and Silver Rock Resort is good for beginners. The Casuarina Beach is also good as the wind is a bit stronger here and funnels down the coast.

Club Mistral has two centres for windsurfing and kitesurfing: **Club Mistral, Oistins**, for intermediate level windsurfers and jump novices, and **Club Mistral, Silver Sands and Skyriders Centre**, for wave novices and experts.

Sports

Kids of all ages will adore Barbados. There is so much to do on the beach and inland that you will never be short of ways to entertain them, even on a rainy day. The compactness of the island means that they won't get bored in a car travelling to somewhere of interest and the lack of large museums and historical buildings means you won't be trailing them around in the heat against their will. The beaches of course are the great attraction, with watersports for all ages on offer and beach bars on hand for refreshments. Many have picnic tables if you want to take your own food and drink. Older children will enjoy a trip on a catamaran up the coast, or there's the fascination of a submarine trip so that they can see what is underwater. Inland, there is the Barbados Wildlife Reserve where they can see monkeys and other animals or they can go horse riding or hiking, and if it rains there is always the cinema. For evening entertainment, teenagers will enjoy the Oistins Friday night fish fry, where there is live music and dancing going on until you drag them home.

Kids' stuff

The water is drinkable, so there are no worries there and generally if you keep them hydrated and avoid sunburn, you won't have any health problems at all. Babysitters usually charge around B$9 per hour.

Eating and drinking

Kids are accepted everywhere although in some of the high class hotels there are restrictions. Food is easy, with plenty of places selling burgers or chicken and chips, while the better restaurants usually have a pasta option. Things are easier if they eat fish.

Sights

Grenade Hall Forest and Signal Station and Barbados Wildlife Reserve, Highway 2, St Andrew, **T** 4228826. *Daily 1000-1700. US$11.50, children half price. To get there take a bus from Bridgetown, Holetown, Speightstown or Bathsheba. Map 2, F5, p216 See also p80* This complex of attractions has something for all the family: animals, history and nature. It can easily absorb half a day during a tour of the north. The Barbados Wildlife Reserve has a huge collection of the large red-footed Barbados tortoise, apparently the largest in the world, which roam slowly around all over the paths, while brocket deer and agouti lounge about in the shade to escape the midday heat. Most of the animals are not caged, you are warned to be careful as you wander around the paths through the trees. There is an architecturally interesting bird house with snakes upstairs and you look down through the metal grid floor to the aviary. The population of the rabbit pen is seriously out of control and the lone wallaby kept with the rabbits and guinea pigs looks stunned. It is an excellent place to see lots of Barbados green monkeys close up if

Kids

they haven't taken off to the forest next door. The primate research centre helps to provide farmers with advice on how to control the green monkeys who are regarded as a pest. The animals are fed near it at about 1600.

The centre has also developed a nature trail in the neighbouring Grenade Hall Forest, with over a mile of coral pathways and interpretative signs. They can be rough, steep and slippery and are definitely not pushchair friendly. Try to be quiet, so as not to disturb birds and animals – a tricky job for kids. Facilities include café and shop and toilets.

Harrison's Cave, Highway 2, St Thomas, close to Welchman Hall Gully, **T** 4386640. *Daily 0830-1630. US$12.50, children US$5. Map 3, A6, p218 See also p70* A visit to the limestone caves involves a 20 minute-train ride on an electric 'train'. You will see some superbly-lit stalactites and stalagmites, waterfalls and large underground lakes. There is a guide to point out the interesting formations and two stops for photo opportunities. Quite educational yet fun for kids.

Harry Bayley Observatory, not far from Banks Brewery, Clapham, St Michael, **T** 4245593. *Fri 2030-2330. US$4, children US$2.50. Map 3, H5, p219 See also p56* The observatory opens to the public once a week. It is the only observatory in the Anglo-Caribbean and is a chance for northern visitors to look through a 14-inch reflector telescope at the Southern Hemisphere stars and planets, which aren't all visible from North America and Europe.

Springvale Eco-Heritage Museum, Highway 2, St Andrew, **T** 4387011, newden@sunbeach.net *Mon-Sat 1000-1600. Sun by appointment. Map 2, J6, p217 See also p92* Springvale is an 80-ha former sugar plantation converted into a folk museum with a presentation of historical rural Barbadian life. The owner will take you around the grounds pointing out the fruits and vegetables and explaining what the herbs are used for. There is a café here too.

Airline offices

Aeropostal, Lower Bay St, Bridgetown, **T** 4361858. **Air Canada**, at the airport, **T** 4285077. **Air Jamaica**, Bayside Plaza, **T** 2286625. **American Airlines**, at the airport, **T** 4284170. **British Airways**, Fairchild St, Bridgetown, **T** 4366413. **BWIA**, Fairchild St, Bridgetown, **T** 4262111. **Caribbean Star**, Lower Bay St, Bridgetown, **T** 4310540. **LIAT**, St Michael's Plaza, St Michael's Row, Bridgetown, **T** 4345428. **Surinam Airways**, Lower Bay St, Bridgetown, **T** 4361858. **Virgin Atlantic**, in Hastings, **T** 1800-744747. Their 'check-in and chill-out' service allows guests at 19 hotels to check in themselves and luggage whilst still at the hotel, so you only need to turn up at the airport 50 mins before take-off, **T** 4362110.

Banks and ATMs

Banks open Mon-Thu 0800-1500, Fri 0800-1700. Banks at shopping centres are usually open Mon-Thu 1000-1900 and Fri 1000-2000. Some open Sat 1000-1500. **Barbados National Bank**, Bridgetown. *Mon-Thu 0800-1500, Fri 0800-1300 and 1500-1700*. There's also a branch and a bureau de change at the airport; the latter is open 0800-2400, but inaccessible unless you are actually arriving or departing. **First Caribbean International Bank**, Bridgetown, south and west coasts. *Mon-Thu 0800-1500, Fri 0800-1300 and 1500-1700*. **Caribbean Commercial Bank**, Bridgetown, south and west coasts. *Mon-Thu 0800-1500, Fri 0800-1300 and 1500-1700*. Branches in Hastings and Sunset Crest. *Sat 0900-1200*. **CIBC Caribbean Ltd**, Bridgetown, south and west coasts. *Mon-Thu 0800-1500, Fri 0800-1300 and 1500-1700*. **Royal Bank of Canada**, Bridgetown, south and west coasts. *Mon-Thu 0800-1500, Fri 0800-1300 and 1500-1700*. **Scotiabank**, Bridgetown, south and west coasts. *Mon-Thu 0800-1500, Fri 0800-1300 and 1500-1700*. Banking facilities in JB's and Big B Supermarkets. *Mon-Thu 1000-1900, Fri 1000-2000, Sat 1000-1500*. There are no banks on the east coast, but the supermarket at Belleplaine has a Royal Bank counter. There is an ATM by the check-in counters at the airport. All banks now have cash machines at most branches where you can use a credit card after hours. There are often cash machines in supermarkets and petrol stations.

Bicycle hire
Flex Bicycle Rentals, **T** 2311518 (mob), **T** 4240321, gmgriff@ sunbeach.net

Car hire
Coconut Car Rentals, Bay Side, Bay St, Bridgetown, **T** 4370297, www.coconutcars.com. One-day rentals from US$86, small cars and mokes for US$121 for 2 days, jeeps from US$133 for 2 days, special offers in summer. Drivers must be over 25 with 3 years' experience. **Courtesy Rent a Car**, airport, **T** 4314160, www.courtesy rentacar.com. Will meet you at the airport, advance phone or internet booking. Drivers must be 21-70 with 3 years' experience. Excellent service, you can have the car delivered to your hotel and drop it off at the airport when you leave. **Eastmond's Car Rentals**, **T** 4287749. Smaller operator, pick-up and delivery, 7 adequate cars, US$288/week including VAT. **Regency Rent-a-Car**, 77 Regency Park, Christ Church, **T** 4275663. Free pick up and delivery. **Stoutes Car Rentals**, **T** 4354456. **Sunny Isle Sixt Rent a Car**, Worthing, **T** 4357979, www.barbadostraveller.com. Will meet you at the airport, advance phone or internet booking. Jeeps and mokes can be can be rented from a number of local firms: **Mohamed**, **T** 4263073, www.mohamedcards.com; **Fat Jack**, **T** 4206502, www.jeep-rentals.com, US$84/day; **ABC**, **T** 4204648, abcrentals@caribsurf.com and others, see tourist brochures for discounts and summer deals.

Credit card lines
American Express, **T** 1-800-3271267. **Mastercard**, **T** 1-800-8472911. **Visa**, **T** 1-800-3077309. For other credit cards without a local contact number, make sure you bring details from home for a number to call if your card is lost or stolen.

Disabled

Most hotels and several of the better guesthouses have rooms adapted for wheelchair users and tour agencies will make arrangements for the disabled to join their island tours. The large catamarans are best for boat tours as they are easier to get on and off. Access to the beach is tricky in a wheelchair but the towns are no more difficult than at home.

Electricity

120 volts (American standard) and 50 cycles per second (British standard). Some houses and hotels also have 240-volt sockets for use with British equipment.

Embassies

Australia (High Commission), Bishop's Court Hill, **T** 4352843. **Belgium (Consulate)** , Rockley Resort, **T** 4357704. **Canada (High Commission)**, Bishop's Court Hill, St Michael, **T** 4283550. **Denmark (Consulate)**, c/o Yankee Garments, **T** 4244995. **France**, Hastings, Christ Church, **T** 4356847. **Germany**, Banyan Court, Bay St, St Michael, **T** 4271876. **Israel (Consul)**, **T** 4264764. **Italy**, **T** 4371228. **Netherlands (Consulate)**, c/o Chickmont Foods, **T** 4188000. **Sweden**, Branckers Complex, Fontabelle, St Michael, **T** 4274358. **UK (High Commission)**, Lower Collymore Rock, St Michael, PO Box 676, **T** 4366694, **US (Consular Section)**, Alico Building, Cheapside, Bridgetown, **T** 4364950.

Emergency numbers

Ambulance **T** 511. Fire **T** 311. Police **T** 211 (enquiries **T** 4366600). Coastguard **T** 4278819.

Gay and lesbian

There are no dedicated gay bars and clubs in Barbados, everyone mixes in together. The most you'll get is something like a Sunday night drag show at Ragamuffins. There are no problems about two people of the same sex booking hotel rooms or hiring apartments. Overt sexual affection is frowned on, but then it is for heterosexuals too as this is a fairly conservative society.

Hospitals

Queen Elizabeth Hospital, **T** 4366450. 600-bed general hospital. Eight polyclinics around the island, Psychiatric Hospital and Geriatric Hospital. **FMH Emergency Medical Clinic**, **T** 2286120. A good private clinic. There are many polyclinics throughout the island.

Internet/email

Bean 'n Bagel Café, St Lawrence Gap, **T** 4204604. *0700-1730*. B$3 for 5 mins, B$10 for 30 mins, B$15 for 1 hr. **Computer Internet Services**, Broad St Mall, Bridgetown. *Mon-Thu 0900-1700, Fri 0900-1800, Sat 0900- 1400.*US$1 for 10 mins, US$6 for 1 hr. **Connect**, just off Broad St, upstairs from Windjammer on Lancaster La opposite Cave Shepherd, Bridgetown, **T** 2288648. *Mon-Thu 0900-1700, Fri 0900-1800, Sat 0930-1430*. US$1 for 7 mins, US$2 for 15 mins, US$7 for 1 hr. Free coffee, student rates with ID, net2phone calls. **Global Business Centre**, West Coast Mall, Holetown, **T** 4326508, www.globalbizcentre.com. *Mon-Fri 0900-1700, Sat 0900-1300*. B$5 for 10 mins, B$0.50 per min thereafter. Also at Quayside Centre on the south coast. **Happy Days**, Chattel Village, St Lawrence Gap. *0800-1500*. B$4 for 15 mins, B$8 for 30 mins, B$12 for 1 hr, B$20 for 2 hrs. **Netcafé**, Sogo Plaza, 20 Broad St, Bridgetown, **T** 4354736. *Mon-Thu 0900-1700, Fri 0900-1800, Sat 0900-1400*. Also in Broad St Mall, Bridgetown, opposite CIBC. US$3 for 15 mins, US$5 for 30 mins, US$10 for 1 hr. **Web Café**, Sunset Crest. *Mon-Fri 0800-2000, Sat-Sun 0900-1700, reduced hours in summer. Turn up by Royal Bank of Canada, parking outside.* B$5 per 15 mins, internet phone calls B$1.50 per min to EU, USA, Caribbean. B$4.50 for normal phone calls, fax B$1 per sheet locally, B$6 abroad, 6 terminals, lots of drinks, friendly service.

Media

The Advocate newspaper also publishes *The Sunday Advocate* and *Sun Seeker*, a fortnightly tourist magazine. *The Nation* also publishes *Daily Nation*, *Midweek Nation*, *Weekend Nation*, *Saturday Sun* and *Sunday Sun*, *The Visitor* tourist fortnightly and the *Barbados Business Authority*, on Monday. *Broad Street Journal* is a free business weekly.

As for radio, there's **CBC Radio**, medium wave 900 kHz; **Starcom Gospel**, medium wave 790 kHz; **BBS**, FM 90.7 MHz; **Love FM**, FM 104.1 MHz; **Radio Liberty**, FM 98.1 Mhz; and **FAITH 102 FM**. There's 1 terrestrial TV channel, **CBC**, which shows mostly US imports, and multi-choice TV with 30 channels and satellite-based **Directv** with 70 channels.

Pharmacies

Pharmacies are generally open 0800-1630 Mon-Sat, 0800-1200 Sun. Look in the local newspapers for pharmacies open at other times, as they change. Prescription medications can be bought from a pharmacy. Supermarkets stock over-the-counter pain killers and things like diarrhoea relief tablets. **Worrels Pharmacy**, Wildey Shopping Plaza, St Michael, **T** 4275468, www.worphar.com. **Jems Pharmacy**, Jamestown Clinic, Holetown, St James, **T** 4326697, delivery service and 24-hr emergency service, **T** 4234721.

Post offices

The General Post Office Headquarters is in Cheapside, Bridgetown and there are district post offices in every parish, open Mon 0800-1500 and Tue-Fri 0800-1515. Local postal rates are B$0.45 for priority, B$0.40 non- priority. Airmail rates to North America are B$1.15 or B$0.45; to Europe B$1.40 or B$0.70; and to the Caribbean B$0.90 or B$0.45. There is an express delivery service of 48 hrs worldwide: to the Caribbean B$28/1 kg plus B$3/500 g extra, USA B$45 + B$8, Europe B$55 + B$12. A Philatelic Bureau issues first-day covers 4 times a year.

Public holidays

New Year's Day, **Errol Barrow Day** (21 Jan), **Good Friday**, **Easter Monday**, **National Heroes Day** (28 Apr), **Labour Day** (1 May), **Whit Monday** (7 weeks after Easter), **Emancipation Day** (1 Aug), **Kadooment Day** (first Mon in Aug), **Independence Day** (30 Nov), **Christmas Day** and **Boxing Day**.

Religious services

Barbadians are a religious people and although the main church is Anglican, there are over 140 different faiths and sects including Baptists, Christian Scientists, Jews, Methodists, Moravians and Roman Catholics. Times of services can be found in *Friends*. **St Michael's Anglican Cathedral**, Bridgetown, **T** 4270790, stmichaels_cathedral@caribsurf.com, www.angelfire.com.ct2/ stmichael, holds Sun services at 0715, 0900, 1100 and 1800. **Nidhe Israel Synagogue**, **T** 427-7611. The Barbados Jewish Community traditional Fri night Shabbat Service is held here at 1930 or at the **Shaare Tzedek Synagogue**, Rockley New Rd, Christ Church. **St Patrick's Roman Catholic Cathedral**, Bay St and Jemmott's La, St Michael, **T** 4262325. Holds Mass on Sat at 1800, Sun at 0700, 0900, 1100 and 1800.

Telephone

Calls from a pay phone cost B$0.25 for 3 mins. Otherwise local calls are free. Many business places will allow you to use their telephone for local calls. International calls can be made from most hotels or, more cheaply, from Cable & Wireless (Wildey). The international code for Barbados is 246. To phone the UK, dial 011-44, the area code without the first 0, then the number; to phone the USA, dial 1, the area code and the number. Faxes can also be sent from and received at C&W. C&W has a public office on the Wharf in Bridgetown for international calls and fax. Phone cards are available for B$10, 20 and 40 from the cruise terminal, phone company offices, and the long list of other outlets; a cheaper way of making overseas calls than using hotel services, and can be used on most English-speaking islands except Trinidad, Jamaica, Guyana, Bahamas. Cellphone rental is US$50 per week, **T** 2340964.

Time
Atlantic Standard Time, 4 hrs behind GMT, 1 ahead of EST.

Tipping
A 10% service charge is usually added to hotel and restaurant bills, but if there is none, a 10% tip is acceptable. Taxis are tipped at your discretion, there is no tipping rate.

Toilets
Not generally a problem as the more popular beaches have facilities and if not, there is usually a beach bar you can use although it helps if you buy a drink. All the main visitor attractions have toilets.

Travel agents
There are dozens of travel agents and tour operators around the island. **Adventure Travel**, Southern Plaza Complex Oistins, Christ Church, **T** 4206037. **American Express Travel Sevices**, PO Box 605C, Horizon House, McGregor St, Bridgetown, **T** 4312423. **Barbados International Travel Services**, McGregor St, Bridgetown, **T** 4312400. **Gem Travel & Tours**, Goding House Spry St, Bridgetown, **T** 4270332. **Horizon Travel**, Fred's Mall, Spry St, Bridgetown, **T** 2283570. **St James Travel**, Sunset Crest Shopping Plaza No 1, St James, **T** 4326725. **Sunny Isle Travel & Tour Company**, Dayton, Worthing, Christ Church, **T** 4358246. **Universal Travel & Tours**, St Michael's Row, St Michael, **T** 4263599. **Value Vacations Travel & Tours**, Hastings Plaza, Christ Church, **T** 4357959. **Windsor Travel**, Hastings Plaza, Christ Church, **T** 4358981. **Worldwide Travel Agency**, Roebuck House, corner Roebuck St and Spry St, **T** 4293701.

A sprint through history

1627 The first English settlers arrive to find an uninhabited island. It had been discovered earlier by the Portuguese, who named it Os Barbados, after the bearded fig trees which grew on the beaches, and left behind some wild pigs. King Charles I gives the Earl of Carlisle permission to colonize the island.

1639 Governor Henry Hawley founds the House of Assembly. Some 40,000 white settlers (about 1% of the population of England) arrive, most of them small farmers.

1643 Commercial production of sugar begins, with plants introduced from Brazil by Dutch Jews, who also bring capital, credit, technology and markets.

1651 After the execution of King Charles I (1649), Oliver Cromwell sends a fleet to take over Royalist Barbados but his forces are held at bay for six months.

1652 The stalemate with Cromwell is resolved with the signing of the Articles of Agreement, later recognized as the Charter of Barbados by the English Parliament.

1650s Sugar Revolution. Most white settlers leave. Plantations are now owned by a small group of whites. African slaves are brought in to work sugar plantations.

1657 Richard Ligon publishes 'A True and Exact History of the Island of Barbadoes...also the principal Trees and Plants There'. He describes the island as "so grown with wood as there could be found no champions (fields), nor savannas for men to dwell in."

1665   Most of the forests are cleared for sugar.

1674   Richard Ford, English surveyor, draws a map of Barbados showing every plantation, 800 sugar mills, water mills and cattle mills, and names of owners. By the end of the 17th century there are over 400 windmills.

1686   Some 100 prisoners deported from England to Barbados after failed Monmouth Rebellion and Judge Jeffrey's 'Bloody Assizes'.

1695-96   Small pox epidemic.

1807   Britain abolishes the African slave trade, but not slavery. Barbados exports locally-bred slaves to other colonies.

1816   Easter Rebellion. Slave uprising in which several hundred slaves are killed when they mistakenly think slavery has been abolished in England. Signal stations subsequently built throughout island to give advance warning of further rebellions.

1833   Emancipation Bill passed by British parliament with slaves to undergo a period of apprenticeship. Barbadian slave owners compensated with average payments of £20 13s 8d per slave.

1838   Slavery abolished with full freedom for apprentices. However, planters carry on as before and newly freed labourers are 'given the choice of starving, working under unsatisfactory conditions, or

Background

	migrating' (Barbadian historian Hilary Backles, *A History of Barbados*).
1840s	Barbadian labourers earn half that of Trinidadians and are the lowest paid in the Caribbean (except Montserrat). Sugar prices fall with greater competition worldwide.
1843	Samuel Jackman Prescod is the first coloured member to be elected to the House of Assembly.
1854	29,727 die in cholera epidemic.
1890s	Severe drought.
1894	Sugar exports are 50,958 tons (8,837 in 1815), 97% of total exports, but market share is declining because of competition from European sugar beet, while half of all plantations are owned by absentee landlords. Capital investment and technological improvement is minimal.
1898	Hurricane devastates island.
1904-14	About 60,000 workers go to Panama to help construct the canal, with 20,000 leaving in 1909 alone.
1908	Yellow fever epidemic.
1919	Drought and flood.
1923	20,000 migrants leave for New York.
1927	Malaria epidemic.
1930s	Effects of worldwide depression felt, with unemployment, falling wages and higher imported

food prices. Infant mortality is 217 per 1,000 live births, compared with 58 per 1,000 in Britain.

1937 Colonial authorities arrest and deport Clement Payne, a trade union organizer from Trinidad who spreads word of labour unrest and riots in neighbouring islands and Marcus Garvey's teachings on pan-Africanism. Riots follow, with police shooting and killing 14, wounding 47 and arresting over 400.

1939-45 Second World War. Reprieve for the sugar industry with the disruption of beet growing in Europe but U-boat activity limits food imports. Rise of the trades union movement and formation of the Barbados Labour Party (BLP), headed by lawyer, Grantley Adams (1898-1971), who represented Clement Payne in his appeal against deportation. West India Royal Commission, chaired by Lord Moyne, produces a damning report on neglect and deprivation in the British Caribbean, describing squalid and unhealthy slums and shanty towns and the dire state of education and health provision.

1940 Colonial Development and Welfare Act authorizes the first funds to be spent on housing and education.

1947 The BLP wins the general elections.

1950 Universal adult suffrage introduced (previously limited to property owners).

1954 Grantley Adams becomes the first Prime Minister of Barbados under a new system of ministerial government.

1955	Hurricane Janet causes severe destruction of infrastructure.
1956	All the British Caribbean islands agree to create the West Indies Federation.
1958	Elections held for the West Indies Federation. Grantley Adams becomes Prime Minister, with headquarters in Trinidad.
1961	Jamaica withdraws from the Federation after inter-island hostility and the whole thing falls apart.
1960s	Rise of tourism with introduction of long-haul jet aircraft.
1966	Barbados becomes an independent member of the British Commonwealth. Errol Barrow of the Democratic Labour Party (DLP) is Prime Minister, 1961-1976.
1986-94	DLP holds office under Prime Minister Erskine Sandiford.
1994-	Barbados Labour Party (BLP) holds office under Prime Minister Owen Arthur.

Art and architecture

17th century

The Jacobean Drax Hall and St Nicholas Abbey are two of the oldest domestic buildings in the English-speaking Americas. At this time many houses were constructed from ballast brought to the island on ships from England, together with local coral stone. Many were destroyed by storms and rebuilt on the same site.

18th century

The oldest ecclesiastical building dates from 1784, only because it was the only one to survive hurricanes, floods and fires. St George Parish Church was destroyed by a hurricane in 1780 and rebuilt four years later. Sugar paid for the construction of grand Georgian colonial mansions and plantation houses built of coral stone and brick ballast in the tradition of the British Empire. The British Garrison, stationed in Barbados from 1780, built hospitals, barracks and houses in the Georgian and Palladian style with grand staircases, arcades and pediments.

19th century

The Victorian style still seen today in churches, rebuilt after hurricanes and other natural disasters, and plantation houses. Verandas were decorated with carved wood tracery, window parapets were trimmed with filigree and sash, and jalousie windows alternated on the façades in perfect proportion. Villa Nova dates from this period, as do the Parliament buildings in Bridgetown. Many chattel houses mimicked the grand houses with their ornate fretwork, carved bannisters and jalousie windows in perfect proportion. Steep gable roofs were designed to withstand heavy winds and rain, fretwork provided shade and a filter against the rain, while jalousie windows, with two sets of vertical hinges and one horizontal, provided maximum protection from the sun and the wind.

20th century
The last plantation house to be built was Francia, in 1910, designed by a Frenchman using a blend of French and Bajan styles with Brazilian hardwoods. With the lessening of British political and cultural influence, and the rise of the USA throughout the Caribbean, more recent architecture is American in style, with office blocks of glass and steel dwarfing the houses on the outskirts of Bridgetown. Many of the hotels along the south coast are concrete blocks.

1900-40
Development of Barbadian art began, with initially a British or European perspective. Pioneer artists battled against a conservative society dominated by the plantocracy, or what was left of it.

1950s
An influx of artists from abroad, considerably influenced the Bajan art scene, arrived and opened it up to new ideas and movements.

1960-
Young Barbadian artists who had left the island to study overseas, returned with new skills and ideas, challenging the established order and keen to develop individual styles and perspectives based on their Afro-Barbadian experiences. The organization and development of art in Barbados has been revolutionized, with a resulting indigenous Bajan vision which is respected worldwide.

Music

In this music mad nation, it is perhaps not surprising that there is a vibrant music industry, with five major recording studios, including Eddie Grant's Ice Label, and another five smaller ones, as well as local manufacturing companies. They turn out recordings by local bands, such as Krosfyah, Square One, Coalishun, the Merrymen and 4D People, as well as international stars such as Mighty Sparrow, Sting and Mick Jagger. As elsewhere, DJs have become cult figures in the nightclubs and on the radio. Look out for names like Jon.Doe, Donnay Da' Mixmasta, Malcolm X and Cindy Rouse.

Calypso

Calypso is the musical form for which Barbados is most famous, although it was originally developed in Trinidad. Calypsonians (or kaisonians, as the more historically minded call them) are the commentators, champions and sometimes conscience of the people. This unique musical form, a mixture of African, French and, eventually British, Spanish and even East Indian influences, dates back to Trinidad's first 'shantwell', Gros Jean, late in the 18th century. Since then it has evolved into a popular, potent force, with both men and women (also children, of late) battling for the Calypso Monarch's crown during Crop Over, Barbados' carnival, see p144. Calypsonians perform in 'tents' (performing halls) in the weeks leading up to the competition and are judged in Pic-O-De-Crop semi-finals, which hones down the list to seven final contenders who compete against the reigning calypso king. Look out for Kid Site, who won in 2004 and 2005. The season's calypso songs blast from radio stations and sound systems all over the islands and visitors should ask locals to interpret the sometimes witty and often scurrilous lyrics, for they are a fascinating introduction to the state of the nation. Currently, party soca tunes dominate although some of the commentary calypsonians are still heard on the radio. There is also a new breed of 'Rapso' artists, fusing calypso and rap music. Chutney, an Indian version of calypso, is also becoming increasingly popular and is also being fused with soca, to create 'chutney soca'.

Mac Fingall is a local calypso singer and entertainer, frequently found at cricket matches (his passion) or the races if he is not MC at Crop Over competitions. His great friend Red Plastic Bag, with whom he has recorded several albums, is also frequently heard around the island. The band which has won most prizes, however, is Krosfyah (formerly called Crossfire), known as the kings of soca and led by Edwin Yearwood, their singer/songwriter who has been a triple crown winner at Crop Over.

Pan music
Pan music has a shorter history, developing in the 20th century from the tamboo-bamboo bands which made creative use of tins, dustbins and pans plus lengths of bamboo for percussion instruments. By the end of the Second World War some ingenious souls discovered that huge oil drums could be converted into expressive instruments, their top surfaces tuned to all ranges and depths (eg the ping pong, or soprano pan, embraces 28 to 32 notes including both the diatonic and chromatic scales). Aside from the varied pans, steel bands also include a rhythm section dominated by the steel, or iron men.

Reggae
Reggae is tremendously popular in Barbados and is played everywhere, all day and all night. David Kirton is probably the leading Barbadian modern roots reggae artist, with several albums under his name since his debut album, Stranger, in 1999. Biggie Irie, a huge singer with a rich mahogany voice, is credited with being one of the key players in the resurgence of reggae bands in Barbados in the 1990s. Reggae jazz saxophonist, Arturo Tappin, has played at every jazz and reggae festival in the Caribbean and has toured the world with big-name artistes. However, Bajans like

to vary their reggae so there is also a fusion of reggae and soca, known as ragga-soca, which has a faster rhythm than reggae but slower than up-tempo soca. Ringbang, created in 1994, is a mixture of all the varied types of Caribbean music with the emphasis on the beat rather than the melody.

Tuk

Tuk is one of the most traditional forms of folk music, having its origins in the slave culture of the 17th century and it is an important means of expression for the black masses in Barbados. It was banned by the English as subversive; plantation overseers believed that the drums were being used to send messages, and it had to wait until after emancipation to resurface officially. Since the revival of Crop Over in 1974, tuk bands have flourished. The instruments used in a tuk band are the kettle drum, bass drum and tin flute, as played by the landship, see p78. There are several school tuk bands as it is promoted among the younger generation to preserve the island's cultural heritage. The music is lively, with a pulsating rhythm influenced by British regimental band music as well as African dances. It is 'jump up' music, used at holiday times and carnival for masquerades, when tuk bands travel from village to village, playing popular tunes and inviting the audience to join in at will.

Musical groups and choirs

Musical groups and choirs include the Barbados Chamber Music Ensemble, the Barbados Symphonia, Sing Out Barbados, the Barbados Festival Choir, Ellerslie Folk Chorale, the Barbados National Youth Orchestra and the Cavite Chorale. There are also numerous gospel groups, including the Nazarene Silvertones, Promise, Gratitude, the New Testament Church of God Chorale, the Wesley Singers, Sister Marshall and Joseph Niles and the Consolers. The Choir of the Cathedral Church of St Michael and All Angels (Bridgetown cathedral) is a mixed choir of 38 choristers: 7 boy trebles, 14 sopranos, 6 altos, 5 tenors and 6 basses. They can be heard every Sunday at Choral Matins (1100) and Evensong (1800) and every first and third Sunday of the month a the Sung Eucharist (0900). Three concerts are performed annually, A Festival of Nine Lessons and Carols for Christmas, Harvest Thanksgiving on the Sunday before Ash Wednesday and A Solemn Music for Good Friday.

Books

Two Barbadian writers whose work has had great influence throughout the Caribbean are the novelist **George Lamming** and the poet **Edward Kamau Brathwaite**. Lamming's first novel, *In The Castle Of My Skin* (1953), a part-autobiographical story of growing up in colonial Barbados, deals with one of the major concerns of anglophone writers: how to define one's values within a system and ideology imposed by someone else. Lamming's treatment of the boy's changing awareness in a time of change in the West Indies is poetic and highly imaginative. His other books include *Natives Of My Person*, *Season Of Adventure* and *The Pleasures Of Exile*.

Brathwaite is also sensitive to the colonial influence on black West Indian culture. Like the St Lucian Nobel Laureate Derek Walcott and others, he is also keenly aware of the African traditions at the heart of that culture. The questions addressed by all these writers are: who is Caribbean man, and what are his faiths, his language, his ancestors? The experience of teaching in Ghana for some time helped to clarify Brathwaite's response. African religions, motifs and songs mix with West Indian speech rhythms in a style which is often strident, frequently using very short verses. His collections include *Islands, Masks and Rights Of Passage*.

In 1942, **Frank Collymore** founded the literary magazine, *Bim*, which gave generations of writers an outlet for their poetry, short stories and literary criticism. Its name was the nickname given to the planters by their slaves. Collymore was not only an editor but also a short story writer with a keen eye for social customs. **Timothy Callender** was first published in *Bim* and is an accomplished short story writer. His collection, *It so happen*, focuses on the Barbadian village and the characters found there. His fictional village is full of eccentrics who he exposes in a series of moral fables. Other Barbadian writers include Austin Clarke, Bruce St John, Karl Sealy, John Wickham, June Henfrey and Geoffrey Drayton.

Fiction

Callender, T, *It So Happen* (1975, paperback 1991), Heinemann. Stories from a fictional village with a cast of characters and rumshop. Has a moral edge and humorous resolutions.

Clarke, A, *The Polished Hoe* (2003), Amistad. Clarke was born in Barbados but emigrated to Canada in the 1950s. This novel is set in the fictional island of Bimshire (Barbados) in the 1950s, where a murder has taken place. Mary-Mathilda, an old woman, confesses in a monologue which takes in her life story encompassing colonialism, racism, servitude and sexual exploitation.

Collymore, F, *The Man Who Loved Attending Funerals and Other Stories* (1993), Heinemann. The founder of the literary magazine, *Bim*, wrote his own stories with a keen, often humorous, observation of society.

Drayton, G, *Christopher* (1959, paperback 1972), Heinemann. A novel of childhood, exploring the gap between the white planter class and the impoverished black, a planter's young son learns about personal relationships and social reality beyond his comfortable and protected world.

Henfrey, J, *Coming Home and other Stories* (1994), Peepal Tree. A collection of short stories about black women and the double oppression of race and gender, including *Freedom Come* about Bussa's rebellion of 1816 and the effect it had on the slaves.

Lamming, G, *In the Castle of My Skin* (1953, paperback 1987), Longman. Another novel about childhood in Barbados, this time from the perspective of a boy growing up in a poor village environment under the oppression of colonial society. His other works include *Native of My person*, *Season of Adventure* and T*he Pleasures of Exile*.

Memoirs

Brathwaite, EK, *Sun Poem*, (1982), Oxford University Press. An autobiographical work in which the author evokes his childhood.

Clarke, A, *Growing Up Stupid Under the Union Jack*, (1980), McClelland and Stewart. A memoir of growing up in Barbados during the Second World War. The author mocks the colonial system of education and traces the move away from Britain towards North America as a role model.

Non-fiction

Cummins, A, et al, *Art in Barbados* (1999), Ian Randle Publishers & Barbados Museum & Historical Society. Examines the work of Barbadian artists over six decades, with beautiful colour reproductions.

Fraser, HS, *Treasures of Barbados*, Macmillan Caribbean. An attractive guide to Barbadian architecture.

Travelogues

Leigh Fermor, P, *The Traveller's Tree, A Journey through the Caribbean Islands.* (paperback 1984), Penguin. A seminal piece of travel writing, perceptive and knowledgeable. Barbados and other islands are written about from the point of view of an outsider, an Irish Englishman in 1947.

Index

Credits

Footprint credits

Editor: Nicola Jones
Map editor: Sarah Sorensen
Picture editor: Rob Lunn
Publisher: Patrick Dawson
Editorial: Sophie Blacksell, Angus
Dawson, Felicity Laughton,
Alan Murphy
Cartography: Claire Benison, Kevin
Feeney, Robert Lunn
Sales and Marketing: Andy Riddle
Advertising: Debbie Wylde
Administration: Elizabeth Taylor
Series development: Rachel Fielding
Design: Mytton Williams

Photography credits

Front cover: Alamy
Inside: Alamy, Pictures Colour Library
Generic images: John Matchett
Back cover: Alamy

Print

Manufactured in India by Nutech
Photolithographers
Pulp from sustainable forests

® Footprint Handbooks and the Footprint
mark are a registered trademark of
Footprint Handbooks Ltd

Every effort has been made to ensure
that the facts in this guide are accurate.
However the authors and publishers
cannot accept responsibility for any loss,
injury or inconvenience sustained by any
traveller as a result of information or
advice contained in this guide.

Publishing information

Footprint Barbados
2nd edition
Text and maps
© Footprint Handbooks Ltd
July 2006

ISBN 1 904 777 58 9
CIP DATA: a catalogue record for this
book is available from the British Library

Published by Footprint Handbooks
6 Riverside Court
Lower Bristol Road
Bath, BA2 3DZ, UK
T +44 (0)1225 469141
F +44 (0)1225 469461
discover@footprintbooks.com
www.footprintbooks.com

Distributed in the USA by
Publishers Group West

Publishing stuff

Acknowledgements

Sarah is very grateful to all those who gave her assistance during her research on Barbados. Thanks go to Petra Roach of the BTA in London and Maggie Gonsalves of the BTA in Bridgetown for organizing and hosting part of her trip there in 2005, as well as Paul Johnson and Anette Ohlsson, of PPC, for their help in arranging accommodation and other logistical issues; to Lynn Girling of The Caribbean Collection and staff at Sunswept Beach Hotel, Southern Palms Beach Resort and Tamarind Cove, and to Uschi Wetzels of Sea-U! Guest House for their hospitality; to Ian Proverbs of Courtesy Rent a Car for car hire; to Peter and Joanne at BWIA for arranging flights; to Chris de Caires, of CWC Barbados for spending a considerable length of time talking cricket and to Brigitte Taylor for a great evening out and advice on the text. Above all, thanks go to Jenny Box for companionship and the tricky business of map reading on Barbados.

Footprint feedback

We try as hard as we can to make each Footprint guide as up to date as possible but, of course, things always change. If you want to let us know about your experiences – good, bad or ugly – then don't delay, go to www.footprintbooks.com and send in your comments.

Complete title list

Africa

Cape Town (P)
East Africa
Eygpt
Kenya
Libya
Marrakech (P)
Morocco
Namibia
South Africa
Tanzania
Tunisia
Uganda

Asia

Bali
Bhutan
Cambodia
Goa
Hong Kong (P)
India
Indian Himalaya
Indonesia
Laos
Malaysia
Nepal
Northern Pakistan
Rajasthan
Singapore
South India
Sri Lanka
Sumatra
Thailand
Tibet
Vietnam

Australasia

Australia
East Coast Australia
New Zealand
Sydney (P)
West Coast Australia

Europe

Andalucía
Barcelona (P)
Belfast & the north of Ireland (P)
Berlin (P)
Bilbao (P)
Bologna (P)
Britain
Cardiff (P)
Copenhagen (P)
Costa de la Luz (P)
Croatia
Dublin (P)
Edinburgh (P)
England
Glasgow (P)
Ireland
London (P)
Lisbon (P)
Madrid (P)
Naples (P)
Northern Spain
Paris (P)
Reykjavik (P)
Scotland
Scotland Highlands
  & Islands
Siena & the heart of Tuscany (P)

Spain
Tallinn (P)
Turin (P)
Turkey
Valencia (P)
Verona (P)

Latin America & Caribbean

Antigua & Leeward
  Islands (P)
Argentina
Barbados (P)
Bolivia
Brazil
Caribbean Islands
Central America & Mexico
Chile
Colombia
Costa Rica
Cuba
Cusco & the Inca Trail
Dominican Republic   (P)
Ecuador & Galápagos
Havana (P)
Mexico
Nicaragua
Peru
Rio de Janeiro (P)
South American Handbook
St Lucia (P)
Venezuela

Middle East

Dubai (P)
Jordan
Syria & Lebanon

North America

New York (P)
Vancouver (P)
Western Canada

Discover guides

Belize, Guatemala & Southern
  Mexico
East Coast Australia
Patagonia
Peru, Bolivia
  & Ecuador
Vietnam, Cambodia
  & Laos

Lifestyle guides

Diving the World
European City Breaks
Surfing Britain
Surfing Europe
Surfing the World

(P) denotes pocket guide

Check out...

WWW...

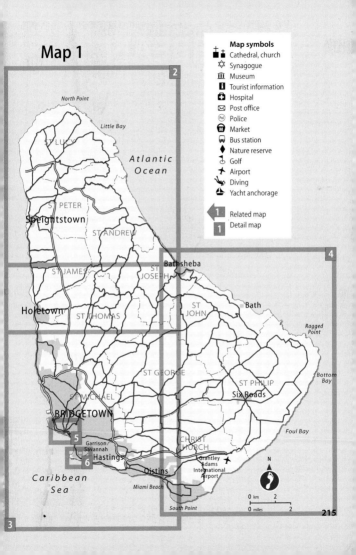

Map 1

Map symbols

- ✝✝ Cathedral, church
- ✡ Synagogue
- 🏛 Museum
- ℹ Tourist information
- ✚ Hospital
- ✉ Post office
- Pol Police
- 🏪 Market
- 🚌 Bus station
- ◆ Nature reserve
- ⛳ Golf
- ✈ Airport
- 🤿 Diving
- ⚓ Yacht anchorage

← 1 Related map

1 Detail map

Atlantic Ocean

North Point

Little Bay

ST LUCY

ST PETER

Speightstown

ST ANDREW

ST JAMES

ST JOSEPH

Bathsheba

Holetown

ST THOMAS

ST JOHN

Bath

Ragged Point

ST GEORGE

ST PHILIP

Bottom Bay

ST MICHAEL

Six Roads

BRIDGETOWN

Garrison Savannah

Hastings

Foul Bay

Caribbean Sea

CHRIST CHURCH

Oistins

Grantley Adams International Airport

Miami Beach

South Point

N

0 km 2

0 miles 2

Map 2

216

Atlantic Ocean

ST LUCY

- North Point
- Archers Bay
- Stroud Point
- Animal Flower Cave
- Harrison Point Lighthouse
- Greenidge
- Maycock's Bay
- Sutherland Road
- Half Moon Fort
- Six Men's Bay
- Port St
- St Lucy's
- Benthams
- Mount Gay Rum Distillery
- Alexandra
- Bishops
- Spring Garden
- The Spout
- River Bay
- Antilles Flat
- St Clements
- Little Bay
- Pie Corner
- Paul's Point
- Gay's Cove
- Pico Teneriffe
- Boscobelle
- Cherry Tree Hill
- St Nicholas Abbey
- Grenade Hall Forest, Signal Station & Barbados
- Morgan Lewis Sugar Mill
- Morgan Lewis Beach
- Farley Hill
- Mile and a Quarter

1 km
0 miles

N

Map 3

1 · **2** · **3** · **4** · **5** · **6** · **7** · **8**

A · **B** · **C** · **D** · **E** · **F**

St Joseph · Horse Hill

Cotton Tower · Surinam Signal Station

Mount Tabor

Villa Nova · Wilson Hill · Wakefield Tenantry

Drax Hall Green

ST GEORGE

Ellerton

Golden Ridge

Parris Hill

Orchid World

Flower Forest

Belair

Gun Hill Signal Station

St George's

Welchman Hall Gully · Harrison's Cave

Jack-in-the-Box Gully

Springvale · Heritage Museum

Welchman Hall

Francia Plantation

Foster Hall

ST THOMAS

Earthworks Pottery

Redmans

Jackson

Endeavour

Rock Hall

St Thomas

ST MICHAEL

National Stadium

Red Clay

Mount Standfast

Porters

Sir Frank Hutson Sugar Machinery Museum

Portvale Sugar Factory

Chattel Village

On the Wall

Folkestone · St James

Holetown

Sunset Crest

Sandy Lane · Folder's House · Polo Field

Thorpes

Fitts

Highway

Spring Garden Highway

Alleynes Bay

Folkestone Park & Marine Reserve

Sandy Lane Hotel · Paynes Bay

Batts Rock Beach

Paradise Beach

West Indies Rum Distillery

Malibu Beach Club

Wine World

Brighton Beach

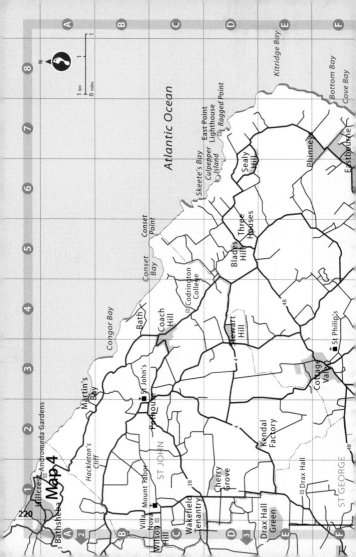

Map 4

A B C D E F

8
7
6
5
4
3
2
1

N

1 km
0 miles

Atlantic Ocean

Hillcrest
Andromeda Gardens
Bathsheba
Hackleton's Cliff
Martin's Bay
Congor Bay

Villa
Mount Tabor
Wilson Hill
Wakefield Tenantry
Cherry Grove
Kendal Factory
Drax Hall Green
Drax Hall

ST JOHN
ST GEORGE

St John's
Bath
Coach Hill
Codrington College
Conset Point
Conset Bay
Skeete's Bay
Culpepper Island
East Point Lighthouse
Ragged Point
Sealy Hill
Blades Hill
Three Houses
Hewart Hill
Cottage Vale
St Philip's
Phinney
Eastbourne
Kitridge Bay
Bottom Bay
Cove Bay

3B
4
4
4B
4B

Map 5 Bridgetown

Lakes Folly

Fontabelle

Emmerton La

School La

Masonhall St

Reed St

Baxters Rd

Lightfoot La

Sobers La

Mahogany La

Tudor St

Central

St Mary's Row

Suttle St

James St

Cheapside

Literary Row

Hart's St

Chapel St

Lukes Alley

Rex Rd

Pelican
Craft Village

Temple Yard

Cumberland St

Lower Broad St

Cowell St

St George St

Mill St

McGregor St

Milk Market

Prince William Henry St

Princess Alice Highway

Prince Alfred St

Hinks St

Zemicon
Gallery

Parry
St

Higginson La

Philade

To Deep Water Harbour

Careenage

N

0 metres   100
0 yards   100